"When I found your books, I was greatly re
and to see that there are Bible-based Christians
ership Education and doing something with it! \
me to take the best of it and work with it. I was primarily using classical method-
ologies, but was fostering a dread of learning by going overboard.

You are the only Christian proponent of this I have been able to find. I am
now sitting down and working out my plan to incorporate all of this new stuff
into my home. I'm looking to others who have similar beliefs and goals who have
gone before me for their input and advice. I want to hear what those who've gone
before me have found useful and not. Your book covers a lot of that."

Leah Jenik (Homeschool Mom)

"Thank you for taking the time to put together valuable training material on
leadership education. I have been homeschooling 6 years and as far as I can see,
there is little-to-nothing available in this area of education that has any practical
application for homechooling parents to use in the mentoring of their children.
Everyone else that I know that home schools is on the conveyor belt to keep up
with the public education counterpart. Thank you for being a "voice in the desert"
that will give guidance to us "many lone horses" that are headed your way."

Cherie, Homeschool Mom

"Thank you so much for being willing to share this "against the tide" information and encourage us to run the race that has been set before us in a Biblical manner.

Dorene Bankester, Homeschool Mom

"I can't tell you how excited I am to read through all of your work. I have
been greatly troubled over the last few months about how our school was going.
I couldn't put my finger on it. And then, providentially, your email about this
book, and I realized that I'm on a conveyer belt. Even with all of my conviction
that I wasn't on that belt, that I had left it, I was completely stunned by the revelation that the public school paradigm still had me in its grips. As a former school
teacher myself, I could so relate to what you were imparting to us. I felt so free
after reading your book. I couldn't stop telling my husband about all the insights I
was having due to your message and influence. I am profoundly grateful to you."

Jodi Guerra, Homeschool Mom

Kerry packs the e-book with tons of practical ideas for implementing a leadership education. . . Grab a highlighter or pen and begin to make specific notes of
how you'll raise leaders...not followers!

Diane Lockman, Classical Scholar &
Author of Trivium Mastery

I believe one of the most important lessons we teach our kids, alongside the "how to think" and the godly character, is being willing to do things differently—even from others who are doing things differently-to hear His voice and follow your specific calling/passion despite the possibility of failure or ridicule. No true leader makes changes in his world without that willingness and courage. Your materials will enable many more to put feet to the raising of leaders.

Lynn, Homeschool Mom

It's really a shame how the public schools are herding their students through the system just to be a clone that will follow the pre-set plan for their lives-a worker that doesn't think for themselves. And they aren't even doing a good job at that, as we hear employers complain that graduates don't even have the basic skills.

Your material is sorely needed for the homeschool community so that Biblically-grounded young adults can re-claim the culture for Christ. It would be nice if the public schools would listen to you too, but we'll just have to dream about that one for now.

Brian, Homeschool Dad

"My husband and I love what we have read so for. When I first began reading about the independent study and mentoring phase I had just finished planning our year and felt discouraged about wasting all that time and effort. As I read further though I was reassured that most of what we have been doing for the past several years have been right on target with the Raising Leaders philosophy (we are in the love of learning stage). It seems as if we have been paddling upstream and just thought maybe we were missing something. As it turns out, paddling upstream is exactly what we need to be doing to raise Godly leaders for our family, community and country. Thanks for the putting together these ideas and forming a peg on which to hang out homeschool philosophy hat!"

Homeschool Mom

"As I have started to go through your book, I realize that there is definitely some shifting I can do this year to improve in a few areas. The Lord was already leading us to focus on some character issues, so it was very encouraging and confirming to see the importance of a good foundation in character in the early years. The one statement you made about the goal being "contemplation", not "productivity" is a golden nugget for me! So, our homeschool focus for the year is now character and contemplation."

Maridel Willer, Speaker & Writer

Raising Leaders, *Not* Followers

A Biblical Perspective of Leadership Education

by
KERRY BECK

Ranger Press
2017

Kerry S. Beck, *Raising Leaders, Not Followers!*

Copyright 2017 by Kerry Beck

Unless otherwise indicated, Scripture quotations are from the New King James Version of the Bible, copyright 1979, 1980, 1982, 1984, 1988 by Thomas Nelson, Inc., Nashville Tennessee.

Ranger Press
How to Homeschool My Child
P.O. Box 4348
Bryan, TX 77805

HowToHomeschoolMyChild.com
Raising-Leaders.com
RangerPress.com

ISBN 978-0-9729913-2-2

Kerry Beck would like to give you a **BONUS Study Guide** & ebook:

Free Study Guide for *Raising Leaders, Not Followers* ($10 value)
http://HowToHomeschoolMyChild.com/leader-study-guide

Everything You Want to Know About Homeschooling **ebook** ($15 value)

You can grab your personal copy here:
http://HowToHomeschoolMyChild.com

Go ahead and pour a cup of coffee & get some chocolate. You'll want to take a coffee break as you read both of these resources. If you want some fun homeschool activities, check these out:

Edible Homeschool:
http://pinterest.com/howtohomeschool/edible-homeschool/

Free Activity Guides
http://HowToHomeschoolMyChild.com/category/activity-guides-2/

TABLE OF CONTENTS

RAISING LEADERS, NOT FOLLOWERS

Children are so excited to start "school", especially when they are young. Let's take a look at two young men who begin their formal schooling.

Two boys prepare for school; excited to go and excited to learn. Creativity is evident in both boys. They like to paint and draw. They like to go out and build forts. They like to make up games for themselves.

Ryan goes off to school. Whether it's a public school or a private school doesn't matter; we see him entering the classroom. Since he wants to be accepted by the teacher and other children, he copies all the other kids. He follows the directions of the teachers. He learns to walk in a straight line.

After a few months, his mom offers him some crayons, and says, "Hey, Ryan, would you like to draw something? Let's sit over here and color together." He sits with her, but doesn't know what to draw. He can't think of anything. He is used to his teacher telling him exactly what to do and when to do it.

Our other friend, Morgan, stays home for school, reading books with his mom. He spends time playing and participating in a variety of activities. Now he doesn't just play all day long. Morgan has small jobs he's able to do at the young age of five or six. He goes to the library every week to pick out books he wants to read. He takes those books home, reads them and talks about them with his mom. She even plans some activities around those books.

Several years go by. Ryan and Morgan are still studying. Ryan is still at the public or private school. He drags himself into the classroom every day. He always does what the teacher tells him. Ryan even reads classics, classics that young kids like to read. He answers the questions on his worksheets and takes tests, making straight A's. He always does his workbooks and turns those in on time. He is learning a ton of information. It's the exact same information as everyone else in the classroom.

Morgan attended a few years of "school" at home. Every day he starts out reading classics with his mom, brothers and sisters. They read them, talk about them, and discuss any lessons that might come from those stories. His mom spends time with him, guiding him through his studies in writing, math and grammar. She helps Morgan along and makes sure he's catching what is necessary. He can speed up when he needs to and he can slow down when he needs to.

A special part of Morgan's "schooling" is the fact that he chooses the topics he wants to study. From there, his mom gears those math and writing assignments around his chosen topic. Our young friend makes projects that he presents to Dad and his siblings. Every week Morgan continues going to the library, picking out those books he wants to read. He has real jobs and real responsibilities. Those responsibilities include jobs around the home and even some responsibilities outside of the home. He's learning to do a job well done.

The years go by and soon they both enter high school. Ryan takes all the right classes to get into college and graduate from high school, but he does not like school. He doesn't feel creative. All Ryan wants to do is get his work done, so he can go play.

When it comes to his education, he learns the same academics and the same subject areas as everyone else. He still reads the classics. Instead of pondering the classics, he listens to what his teachers say about those classics and takes the tests. He gets his answers correct, according to what his teachers have told him. When it comes to arguments and logic, he can pull them apart and tell you what's right or wrong with them. But, Ryan has a difficult time making wise decisions. He spends his evenings at home, it's usually in front of the TV because he's done with his schoolwork .

Morgan has a different high school experience in that he chooses his studies, according to what interests him. His classes include a variety of learning techniques - online classes or classes that his mom mentors him. The number one resource Morgan uses for all of his classes is a real book--reading the classics. When he reads those books, he writes about them and the lessons that he learns from them.

Each week his mom has discussions about the different areas that he's studying. Sometimes they get into long discussions. Sometimes they're short discussions. Sometimes those discussions are continued at the dinner table when Dad is home. Their goal is to look at Morgan's studies from a Biblical world view, so he uses a Biblical perspective with his history study, math study or science study.

His parents are his mentors, but Morgan also shadows a doctor in town because his parents want him to have real life experience. They want him to make his own decisions about his future. One reason he makes these decisions is because he has real responsibility growing up and opportunities to think on his own. Not only does he helps around the home, he has a part time job at the local grocery store. He learns responsibility by using his money wisely.

These two stories exemplify two different approaches of teaching children today. I believe one of those kids will become a better leader because he has learned "how" to think, not just "what" to think. Morgan is not told what the books mean, nor does he take tests according to his teacher's conclusions. He actually reads books and discusses them with his parents.

Both young men have parents who truly want the best for their children, but one parent follows what they experienced growing up. They offer a conveyor belt education; the other offers a leadership education.

Morgan has a parent who reads the same books, take an interest in his interests and discusses the issues. It doesn't matter if his interests are history, literature, auto mechanics, math, motorcycles, or X-box. No matter what, he's a young man who makes decisions in his life and wrestles with life issues. Our young friend is not treated like a container where we pour in that information. Morgan receives "leadership education"; I hope to share ways you can offer your children a similar education.

LEADERSHIP
EDUCATION

WHAT IS A LEADER?

Leadership education is a process of raising our children to be leaders of the future, leaders in business as entrepreneurs, leaders in the church as elders or deacons, leaders in the community as statesmen who do the right thing. These are the leaders who will make a change in our society. My hope for my own children is they will be the leaders of the future.

You may wonder why one child gets an education to become a leader and another receives training to follow. The best way I can summarize the reason why is that a child who learns how to think will become the leader of tomorrow. When a young man or woman can think outside the box, when they can think on their own, when they can take the Scriptures and apply the Scriptures to real life situations, then he will become the leader of tomorrow, rising to do what is right thing.

According to Jeff Myers a leader has strategic vision, strategic mission and strategic motivation. Let's take a look at each one of these aspects of a leader so you understand leadership education for your.

STRATEGIC VISION

Strategic vision is keeping an eye on the big picture, not getting caught up in managing the details. A leader is not a manager. Managers rely on systems and controls to accomplish tasks. Leaders, on the other hand, rely on their vision for the future to keep them focused on what is important. They use that vision to motivate those under them. Leaders are innovators and creators that rely on the people around them to bring about their goals.

To cast the vision to those around them, leaders must have a clear idea of their own vision. Then, they can offer guidance and direction to the

> *Where there is no vision, the*
> *people perish*
> ***Proverbs 29:18***

group they are leading. To do so, your young leader must know how to think and solve problems. Offering real direction to others comes not from rules and systems, but from a strategic vision.

Too often, we raise our children to learn all the rules without giving them the tools to apply rules to the vision set before them. It is imperative that leaders accept the vision and model it. When a leader models the vision, the group responds and it becomes a reality to everyone.

Churchill says, "If you are doing big things, you attract big men. If you are doing little things, you attract little men. Little men cause trouble". More often than not, we think too small and are afraid of risk. Leaders must think big to do big

> *If you are doing big things,*
> *you attract big men.*
> *If you are doing little things,*
> *you attract little men.*
> *Little men cause trouble.*
> *~ **Winston Churchill***

things. When your children have the attitude of fulfilling big things, they will work with others who are like-minded. If their vision is small, they will work with others who think small.

A fellow homeschool mom shared this idea to develop the idea of doing big things as you model for your own children.

> *Start with something BIG, but not radical. For instance,*
> *change your learning space so the kids notice this is going*
> *to be different, particularly if you've been encountering*

resistance in your homeschool, but don't try to purge in the same week (or even month) and spend hours on end reading classic after classic. It's very tempting to implement all the changes immediately because you get so excited, but if you do everything at once, you'll probably overwhelm everyone in your family. Good luck and God bless!

- Patti Wykoff

From my own experience, men are afraid of failure so they don't even try to make a change. This goes for homeschool parents, too. If you are afraid your children will not reach the government's demands, you will not try a new approach to your homeschool.

Think about this for a moment. Who knows best what your children need as they grow up in your home: you or the local public school board?

God has given you everything you need to prepare your children to be godly adults who can follow Him all the days of their lives. If you want your children to grow up to lead and take risks, you must model leadership for them. An easy place to start is in your homeschool. Make a single change in your homeschool that can equip your children to learn how to think Biblically. The courage you exhibit to make this change will set an example of leadership for your children.

Next, put your kids in a situation where they must take risk. It doesn't have to be huge risk, just a place where they show courage in taking that risk. Examples of taking a risk may include trying out for a sports team or a part in a play.

Since your children are in your home, you can guide and encourage them through this situation. When they succeed, praise them for their success and willingness to take a risk. Spend time discussing what they did and why they were successful.

If they fail, show them how to learn from their mistakes. Parents forget that you can learn much more from failures than successes. One thing I tell my children is they can't make the same mistakes as me. They must make new mistakes. From this, we all learn at the same time.

To be honest, I was not good at letting my kids fail. When Ashley tried out for the high school basketball team, I encouraged her to quit tryouts because I didn't think she would make the team. It's one of those decisions I am embarrassed to share with you. I wish I had let her finish tryouts because we never knew if she would make the team or not. As a parent, it is difficult to watch your children not succeed, but it is very important that you encourage them and guide them in the lessons God wants them to learn.

On the other hand, I've watched my son, Hunter, take risks in his job. He turned down two projects because they were not in the area of his interest. Hunter took a risk and trusted God to provide the right project. Within a week, he had two project managers say they would hire him for their next project. This past week Hunter was placed on one of those projects, traveling to Philadelphia each week.

Taking a risk should not be for the sake of being risky. It should be a risk with God's direction in your life. It's the perfect opportunity to learn trust in God while stepping outside the box.

Risk takers are in short supply these days. Ones with a Godly strategic vision are gold. Risk-taking leaders will make changes for the good!

STRATEGIC MISSION

God has gifted each of your children individually to fulfill their strategic mission. Spend time praying about the gifts God has given each of

> *for the gifts and the calling of God are irrevocable*
> **Romans 11:29**

your children so you encourage those gifts in each child. Talk to your children about their strengths so they will start using those gifts in ministering to those around them. Romans 11:29 tells you, *"for the gifts and the calling of God are irrevocable".*

Leaders know their strategic mission and work to fulfill it. As parents, you need to develop those areas in each child's life. John Maxwell says it well, "Find the one thing that you believe is the potential leader's greatest asset, and then give 101 percent encouragement in that area".

STRATEGIC MOTIVATION

Finally, leaders are motivated to fulfill their vision and mission. Watch to see what your children truly enjoy doing as they grow to work independently. What lights their fire? What do they do when given free time? These are the activities they are motivated to accomplish.

Let's face it, sometimes your children want to pursue jobs or ministry that you aren't too crazy about. I can relate, can you?

Last year, Ashley was offered a part time job at her church, but I thought it might take away from her job as mom & wife. I was completely wrong. It was the best decision Ashley could have made because it gave her purpose working with young kids. She developed friendships with spiritual leaders that were able to mentor her through difficult times that God put in her life.

Some parents worry about their children being able to get a "good job" so they discourage mission work, art, music careers or similar pursuits. If God has given your child the gifts to pursue a specific mission, you should be open to where God is leading, not where you are moving. As parents, try not to criticize these pursuits until much prayer has been poured over it.

Sometimes your goals for your child's career are an extension of the conveyor belt mentality which follows the crowd. I grew up on that conveyor belt just like you, so watch out when it creeps into your thought process. Think outside the box to encourage your child as he become motivated in God's direction of his life.

OVERVIEW OF LEADERS IN TRAINING

The quality of questions you ask determines the quality of your life, according to Andrew Kern, of Circe Institute. Leaders-in-training learn to ask the right questions. They do not simply think on literal terms; they think beyond the literal, evaluating and analyzing issues. They become good decision-makers.

When questions are asked, decisions must be made. As your students answer questions, they develop the habit of making good decisions. Continue asking questions so your kids continue practicing good decision making.

Sometimes good decisions must be made with the mentor's guidance. Therefore, give your students plenty of practice answering questions with you at their side. Classics are a great place to start your questioning.

The essence of thinking is asking & answering questions. The discussion that ensues develops character in your children. Asking questions will eventually develop wisdom and train your children to think with virtue and justice. There is a difference between thinking "with virtue" and thinking "about virtue". Strive to have your children use virtue in all aspects of their lives. Consider which questions drive you forward to thinking with virtue and justice. This will be your guide as you choose questions to ask your students.

In addition to developing good decision making skills, your leader-in-training will learn to contemplate difficult issues when asked questions. Our society is bent on production as being the end point. God has a different view.

> *Get wisdom! Get understanding!*
> *Do not forget, nor turn away from the words of my mouth.*
> *Do not forsake her, and she will preserve you;*
> *Love her, and she will keep you.*
> *Wisdom is the principal thing;*
> *Therefore get wisdom.*
> *And in all your getting, get understanding.*
>
> **Proverbs 4:5-7**

Wisdom is God's ultimate goal for your children, not productivity. Although God wants us to be productive for Him, He wants us to grow in wisdom more so. Wisdom is the main thing! Start asking your children questions at an early age, so they will develop wisdom under your guidance.

Asking questions & decision making can be as simple as letting your child choose which clothes they are going to wear or what your family has for dessert tonight. You can then move past simple questions & decisions, to asking their opinion of who might win March Madness or the Presidency. Decisions do not have to be super-serious all the time. Discussing who will win the basketball game in tonight's March Madness game can generate as much decision making as who will win the race for President. As your kids discuss either of these questions, they will begin making decisions.

To help your kids grow in making decisions, asking questions and contemplating issues, you should model these ideas as well. You should grow in decision making and question asking. Here are a few concrete ideas for you to grow as a leader.

PERSONAL GROWTH PLAN

Jack Welch says, "Before you are a leader, success is all about growing yourself. When you become a leader, success is all about growing others". That sums up what you as a homeschool mom should be doing. First, you grow yourself. Next, you grow your kids. A personal growth plan starts with you.

Another aspect of personal growth plans is the necessity of reading. Most books about leadership come to the same conclusion, "To lead, you must read". Leaders continue to learn throughout their lives. Reading is natural for leaders because they want to learn more and more in their

>
> *To lead, you must read*

areas of expertise. Thus, a personal growth plan is imperative. I'd like to give an overview of a personal growth plan. Your kid's personal growth plan is explained in my book, *Teach Your Children "How to Think" with Mentoring*.

Remember modeling is the best way for your kids to learn. Have you ever noticed that your kids have similar mannerisms as you or your spouse? That's because they mimic everything you do. So, let them mimic you in education as you develop your own personal growth plan. When you model the importance of a personal growth plan, your children pick up on its importance.

Set Aside Time

In *A Thomas Jefferson Education,* Oliver DeMille suggests that older students who work independently should choose a specific time during the day to study. Structuring the time encourages ownership and leadership in the student's education. The same is true for parents.

> **Personal Growth Plan**
> – *Set Aside Time*
> – *File Quickly What You Learn*
> – *Apply Quickly*
> – *Share with Others*

So start your personal growth time by choosing a time each day for study. For our family, we chose the mornings. Mornings were set aside for group study & individual study, depending on the kids' ages.

For my personal growth plan, I set aside early morning. Each morning I would wake up before my family so I could read my Bible & other books. This was also my time to journal. Mornings are still the best time for me to study.

What about you? What time each day will you spend reading & thinking? What about your kids? When will they read & discuss what they are learning?

When you structure the content by giving your students a checklist, you teach bureaucracy, bringing the public or private school mentality to home. Most public and private schools are set up like a factory. Students are expected to cover the exact same material at the exact same grade level as everyone else. This set-up is similar to a factory that sends raw goods down a conveyor belt, stopping at 12 different stations (grade levels). Once the conveyor belt stations are completed, you have a finished product a (graduate) who is ready for the market (the job market).

Students who complete this type of training learn how to follow and obey orders well. They seldom learn to how to think or solve problems. Graduates of the American, factory-type schools are highly-trained, but poorly educated. Historically, societies like ours eventually lose their freedoms. Unfortunately, most Americans are so entrenched in this type of thinking they don't even realize how many freedoms they have lost in recent generations.

To develop leaders, you must leave the checklist mentality and set aside ample time to study. During this study time, you allow your students an opportunity to choose content areas based on their strategic vision, mission and motivation. As your student pursues those areas, you encourage his education instead of simply training him for a job. Your expectations should be reasonable, depending on your student's age, strengths and weaknesses.

File Quickly What You Learn

Several methods can be used for you and your children to file quickly what they learn. Let me share a few that our family used during our years of homeschooling.

When they are young, they can use a copybook. Mom chooses a few sentences to copy from the book they are reading. Copywork reinforces the

> *File Quickly*
> – *Copywork*
> – *Commonplalce Book*
> – *Reading Journals*
> – *Note Cards*
> – *Phone Apps*

concepts they are learning in a variety of subject areas: Literature, Bible, History, Geography, Science, Music, Art and so forth.

A commonplace book has been used for centuries and is another way your kids can record quickly what they learn. Did you know you can still read our founding fathers' commonplace books? In following the commonplace book example, students record quotes and comments from his studies in a commonplace book. This may come from readings, lectures, sermons, or even movies. Commonplace books can also be used as a resource for your student's writing assignments. Examples to support their thesis are often found in commonplace books.

Reading journals can be used at all ages. Younger children will write about the story they read or heard. If they are unable to write easily, let them draw pictures of what happened in a story. Older students should write about the lessons or ideas they learn from a specific readings. Daily reading journals are an excellent way for moms to discover what a student is learning from his readings.

Note cards are another method your students can use to file quickly what they learn. This reminds me of the note cards I used when doing a huge research paper in high school. I found this method works well as we study specific topics. As I've studied leadership, I've kept note cards about a variety of sub-topics. For each sub-topic, I have an index card where I record any details I want to remember in the future. Since they are on note cards, I can sort & re-sort the topics to fit my workshop outline, article, book, blog post or other presentation I am giving.

Moving into the age of technology, I've use a few apps on my phone to record quickly what I learn. Since my phone is usually with me, I can pull up an app during a sermon, while watching television, or listening to a podcast. I can write down what I am learning for future reference. One of my favorite apps is Evernote because it has a search function. When I want to look up notes about a specific topic, I can search all my notes for that keyword.

As a word of caution, I do not recommend computers, phones, ipads for most recording. I still handwrite in my journal each day what I am learning. Yes, I am still on a personal growth plan even though my kids have graduated. I plan to be on a personal growth plan for my entire life.

There is something special about writing with your hand. It forces you to think what you are recording. When students type notes, they generally take dictation trying to record everything they are learning. The thought process while writing by hand is essential for critical thinking skills. I recommend sparingly using "screens" to record what is learned.

These are just a few of the methods our family uses to record quickly what we learn in our readings and studies. See what works best for your family and your individual children. You may need to use a variety of methods, depending on your strengths and weaknesses.

Apply Quickly What You Learn

What makes a successful leader? They are able to communicate their vision and the lessons they are learning to others. Give your children opportunities to present the lessons they are learning as they prepare to be a leader.

You can begin with Bible study or family devotions. As you read the Bible together, discuss lessons you want your children to learn. From those lessons, you can hold your kids accountable. As you work through these Biblical lessons, you might consider memorizing verses to reinforce the lesson.

From there, show your children how they can apply other areas of study. When they learn something cool in Science, Math, History or other subject areas, have them share it with someone in their family. Next, they can share it with a friend. Finally, they should teach the discovery to someone else. By following this method, even young students can learn to share their new-found knowledge and teach it to others. Not only does this provide opportunities to practice leadership skills, it also offers many chances to learn thinking skills. Your child should communicate their new-found knowledge, he or she will also learn how to think more clearly.

Don't forget, you are to model this for your children to follow. When you read and learn something really interesting, share it with your family. At times, my son learns more from us talking about a topic in the car than from the books he reads.

Most of all, your personal growth plan should include growing in your relationship with God. Use the ideas above for both you and your children as you read and listen to the Bible.

> *Set aside time for growing in God*
> *Write down the lessons you learn from God*
> *Apply those lessons in your life*
> *Share what God is teaching you with others.*

When should you start your personal growth plan? Today! You need to start today. Take a few minutes and plan your personal growth plan. Don't wait until you need a growth plan. At that time, it is too late. When you wait too long, you lose opportunities for a relationship with your kids. You lose opportunities to instill a love of learning and encourage thinking skills in your children.

If you are too old or too busy to have a personal growth plan, you are too busy to parent and mentor your children. I can guarantee the timing is never perfect, so start immediately. You don't have to start perfectly, you just need to start.

When you follow a personal growth plan, you make an investment in yourself and your children. I can not emphasize enough the importance of life-long learning with a growth plan. When you and your children continue to grow, you continue to develop thinking skills in all areas of life. Personal growth is not memorizing facts and re-telling them on a test. Personal growth is applying those concepts you learn.

We often get learning and thinking confused. Einstein was once asked how many feet are in a mile. His reply was quite interesting. "I don't know. Why should I fill my brain with facts I can find in two minutes in any standard reference book." You can learn a huge lesson from Einstein. It is more important to use your mind to think, than as a warehouse of facts. Unfortunately, the conveyor belt trains their students to use their mind as a warehouse of facts. You have the opportunity to show your children how to use their mind to think.

READ – WRITE - DISCUSS

Before moving on, I want to discuss the idea of read-write-discuss in more depth. The best way I know to encourage excellent questions and train our children how to think on their own is have them read, write and discuss. Students who read, write and discuss have a broader education than someone who simply learns the right answers to questions. Just because you read a classic, doesn't mean you actually ponder the lessons of that classic or discuss the issues at hand. Writing and discussing are very important in developing critical thinking, as well as training your children to be leaders. These two activities force students to mull over the text.

Children who go through this type of education discuss issues as a family. A great place for family discussions is the meal table. Of course, this assumes your family eats meals together and discusses a wide variety of topics. Family discussions should run through the grid Scripture and what God has to say about those issues.

> *Meal-time discussions provide ample time for parents to mentor their children*

Let me be clear about one thing – I am not talking just about theology discussions around the dinner table. These discussions include issues in your church, issues in your community, issues in the world, and discussing those issues from a Biblical worldview. A great place to start discussions is centered on the book your family is reading together. Having meal-time discussions provide ample time for parents to mentor their children and provide a strong leadership education.

Follow the grid of Scripture in your discussions. Whatever you are discussing should come from a Biblical worldview. As you mentor your kids in a Biblical worldview, you begin to develop Christian leaders.

In order to win our society for Jesus Christ, we need Christian leaders who can impact the world for Him. As our children become future leaders, they must learn to use a Biblical worldview as they study. Realizing Christ is the center of all areas of life is essential for young men and women. Christ is not just the center of Bible and history, but Math, Science, Art, Music. The leaders who make a difference with American society, whether good or bad, will be students who are educated to be leaders. Why not train your children to be the best leaders they can be and make a positive change in our society for Jesus Christ?

Creating a positive change for Jesus Christ is not merely found in church, in ministry or in overseas mission work. Christian leaders exist in all areas of life—in the business world, in the medical field, in the legal field, at the utilities company, at work downtown at the coffee shop – all of these can change society. We need leaders in every aspect of society to improve America and bring it back to Christian roots. Too often Christians rely on their pastor to solve the world's problems, but God wants us all to be faithful in our daily endeavors so we can influence the world for His kingdom.

If you want to know more about this process of read-write-discuss, I recommend my book, *Teach Your Children How to Think with Mentoring.*

SUCCESSFUL LEADERSHIP EDUCATION

You might wonder, "If I follow this model of read-write-discuss, how will I know if I'm successful?" I encourage you to take a few minutes before you read any further and contemplate success.

What does a successful education mean to you and your family? Decide what success for your children means to you, not the public school or your homeschooling neighbor. Take out a piece of paper and write it down. What will your child look like if he is successful through a leadership education approach? Think for awhile before you read further.

For myself, I have a few lifelong goals for my children. First, I want them to think on their own. I don't want them to just listen to their teachers or church leaders, soaking everything in as the truth. I want them to use Scripture to back up their ponderings. To sum up my first goal, I want my children to think Biblically and critically throughout their lives.

Next, I want my children to make wise decisions. They must have solid, mature character in order to make enlightened decisions. In addition to strong character, I want my children to understand what freedom is, as well as enjoy freedom in their own lives. Most Americans are slaves and don't even know it. They are slaves to their jobs, slaves to their school, and especially slaves to the government.

In America today, we often do not have the opportunity to make decisions on our own. We have rules and regulations for all areas of life – how to drive (with a seat belt), how fast to drive (speed limits), what type of medicines to buy (approved by FDA), what textbooks to use in schools (state approved), and how much we owe in taxes for owning our home (property taxes). The list goes on and on. We are so used to living according to the government rules, we don't even realize there may be another way to live. Few people in the world today live the way they want. I want my children to understand what freedom is and strive for more freedom in their lives, as well as their children's lives.

> *A successful leader reproduces himself in his followers. There is no real success without a successor*

Another way to view success is to consider the idea of reproducing yourself. A successful leader reproduces himself in his followers. There is no real success without a successor. As you model and mentor your children, they will reproduce you. Reproduce your hand gestures. Reproduce your words. Reproduce your thoughts.

This puts a heavy burden on you to be a good example for your children. Thankfully, God gives you the strength and ability to raise your children well. Rest in Him as you develop your children into leaders for the future.

> *Rest in the Lord & wait patiently for Him.*
> **Psalm 37:7**

LEADERS CHANGE COMMUNITIES

Personally, I believe the greatest place we can change America is in our neighborhoods and the business world. Communities have lost touch with neighbors, as they live independently and individually. On the other hand we can change the norm by sharing God when we meet and enjoy your neighbors.

Sharing God takes place in both your words and your actions. Actions do speak louder than words. Our family took meals to many families, including those with a newborn, those home from the hospital, or those who lost a loved one. My kids helped me prepare the meal by making the dessert. They loved baking. They also helped me deliver the meal. What an easy way to teach your children to serve others. When you take a meal to someone in need, you speak volumes to that family. Serving others should be a natural part of your lives as your children grow up. Community leaders reach out in simple ways and make a difference.

Businesses influence how communities run on a daily basis. When decisions are made in a town, the large businesses have a say in what will be done. It is amazing how quickly city officials listen to the big taxpayers of the town, the entrepreneurs. On a larger scale, why do you think Congress listens to Bill Gates about specific issues? Bill Gates has the money and power to be heard. But, Bill Gates didn't start as Microsoft, he started as a small business. You don't have to be as big as Microsoft to impact the world. Small businesses are still the backbone of America and continue to impact their communities.

Local entrepreneurs think for themselves and make changes in the world around them. One of our family's goals is that our children have the ability to become entrepreneurs if they desire it. They will not be dependent on an employer for their income and will have the freedom to live as God directs them. As an entrepreneur they can make wise decisions and lead those around them. One of our companies, FamilyEbiz.com helps families gain freedom and control over their lives.

Another goal is to change America for the good, one small business at a time. As small family businesses grow, they can have an impact on their own town. Christians can impact their world through businesses, possibly more than church ministries. Why not train your children to be leaders in business that will impact the world for the kingdom of heaven?

A WORD OF CAUTION

Before I go on to the "nuts and bolts" of how you can implement leadership education, I need to offer a word of caution. If you follow this approach, you will be different from those around you. It will be hard at times and I can empathize with any difficulties you may encounter. Pray and trust God that you are making the decisions for your children. When you are in the palm of His hand, you know you are doing the right thing.

> *There is only one form of political strategy in which I have any confidence, and that is to try to do the right thing*
> *-Calvin Coolidge*

I know it will be difficult because that's how I feel a lot of times. I am the odd one because we "do" think on our own. I use Scripture to support my decisions, as well as my prayers. I train our children to do the same. As your children grow into leaders, they might take a stand for the "right action" because the Bible supports it. If you are taking a stand for the right thing now, you know how difficult this is. So, you should be able to empathize with your children in the future. It can be heart-breaking to watch your children not fitting into all the groups around them, even in church.

The Lord is near to those who have a broken heart,
    And saves those who are crushed in spirit.
                                              Psalm 34:18

Rest assured, when you use Scripture as your grid for making decisions, you have God on your side. He will support you to the end.

There is only one form of political strategy in which I have any confidence, and that is to try to do the right thing - and sometimes be able to succeed.
            - Calvin Coolidge (1872-1933)

Calvin Coolidge was one of the "coolest" presidents I studied (pardon the pun). He was an upright man who strove to do the right thing, even in the face of adversity. Are you doing the right thing when you raise your children to be godly leaders? You may face trials along your way – in-laws, government officials, neighbors, but God will see you through as you follow His lead.

If you have a spouse that's on board, that's great. If not, begin praying for you and your spouse. Changes won't necessarily happen overnight. Remember, God is faithful. One time I spent years praying for Steve about an area in our lives. Notice I did not see days, weeks, or months. It took years before I saw a change in Steve and me, as well as a resolution in this matter. I learned a great lesson with this matter. Although we live in an instant society (instant pudding, instant oatmeal), God is not an instant God. He takes time to change us into the person He wants us to be. If God hasn't answered your prayer in a matter of months, give it some time. Give Him years to work in you or your spouse. A praying spouse will bring about change in a family. Don't give up!

Sometimes families appear to have similar goals because they use similar vocabulary. For example, many families want their children to learn *how to think*. When you toss around the term, *how to think,* it appears you are on the same wavelength. Unfortunately, that is not always the case.

In my own experience, some families believe that teaching a logic class, using a fallacy book or learning rhetoric will teach their children how to think. These can be tools, but they do not teach *how to think,* in and of themselves. The best way to encourage independent thinking is to have opportunities for discussion and expressing their opinions; opportunities to make decisions; and opportunities to lead others Be aware that leadership education encompasses more than the study of logic and rhetoric. It requires discussion of issues, asking quality questions, making decisions and leading others.

YOUR EDUCATION PARADIGM

In the next pages, I want to provide you with hands-on ways to get started with leadership education. Then, I will discuss working with younger children, establishing godly character and creating a love of learning. Following that, I conclude with practical ideas as you shift towards independent studies. The final stage in leadership education at home is independent studies. To learn more about independent studies and mentoring your kids, I suggest my book, *Teach Your Children How to Think with Mentoring.*

If you want to begin with only one change in your homeschool, I encourage you to change your own education paradigm. For now, I'd like to share a bit about education paradigm. Then, I will continue to build on education paradigm throughout this book. This helps you make a smooth transition to raising your children as leaders.

"What in the world do I mean by education paradigm?"

Most of us grew up in a public or private school, which can be likened to a factory. All the students come to the factory or the school. They start in kindergarten and move on to first grade, down the conveyor belt as Oliver DeMille describes in *A Thomas Jefferson Education.* At each stage of the conveyor belt (or grade level), the student learns the exact same information as everyone else. The students are told what to think. Even though a school may use tools like classics, the school's approach to education only teaches children "what to think".

Too often, teachers lecture and "force-feed" information to their students. I do not believe lectures are bad; they have a place. But too often, teachers lecture, telling their students what to think about the readings. Later on, tests are given to determine if the student knows what the teacher thinks about the readings, not what the students discover about the readings. John Gatto says it well.

> *After you fall into the habit of accepting what other people*
> *tell you to think, you lose the power to think for yourself.*
> **John Taylor Gatto,** *A Different Teacher, 2002*

Gatto's statement is strong, and valid! When you have a steady diet of lecture, you lose the power to think for yourself. This summarizes much of the government schools today.

In the American factory schools, all students move from kindergarten through the twelve stages on the conveyor belt. They get stamped with a diploma, ready for the job market. Some move on to college where you find a similar approach to education. Students jump on the college treadmill, making choices about what they want to study. After students choose a field of study, they are told exactly what classes to take. This allows no freedom; it allows no personalization; it allows no opportunity for students to learn how to think on their own. Neither does it allow much discussion for students to use their brain, contemplating a particular issue and growing in wisdom or virtue.

Unfortunately, high level employees are not looking for that type of training. Let me share a story about the President of a growing company as he responded to a very intelligent (by the school's measure) young man. This guy answered all the questions on a quiz show correctly for several weeks. The questions covered a wide variety of subject areas. After answering an odd question about an Argentina mountain, the president commented, "How much do you think I'd pay that guy to work for me?"

"How much?" his guest asked.

"Not a cent over $300 – not per week, not per month, but for life. I've sized him up. That 'expert' can't think. He can only memorize. He's just a human encyclopedia, and I figure for $300 I can buy a pretty good set of encyclopedias. In fact, maybe that's too much. Ninety percent of what that guy knows I can find in a $2 almanac."

"What I want around me," he continued, "are people who can solve problems, who can think up ideas. People who can dream and then develop the dream into a practical application; an idea man can make money with me; a fact man can't."

> *What I want around me are people who can solve problems, who can think up ideas. People who can dream and then develop the dream into a practical application; an idea man can make money with me; a fact man can't.*

Throughout the next several chapters I will offer ideas about your education paradigm, your dreams, your creativity. We'll look at specific steps to help you decide your own paradigm. Take your time. Pray for God's wisdom. Write down your thoughts as you come to conclusions.

KNOW, GLORIFY & ENJOY GOD

Virtue and wisdom are necessary for leaders to lead well. To cultivate wisdom and virtue, you must nourish your children's souls on truth, goodness and beauty. As your kids contemplate these concepts in life or the books they read, be intentional with your interactions. Introduce your children to what is true, what is good and what is beautiful. As your kids get older, you should see them becoming more virtuous and wise in all areas of life. Obviously, this is the goal of education.

But nurturing their souls in truth, goodness and beauty is not enough for our future Christian leaders. "Without a vision, the people perish" (Proverbs 29:18) is just as true for homeschoolers, as it is for the church. Homeschoolers need a vision of where they are headed with their children.

If you do not have the end goal in mind, you can not make wise decisions along the way.

For my kids, the final goal in education would be young adults who know, glorify and enjoy God. When your children conclude their education at home, they should know God fully, glorify Him in all they do and enjoy Him forever. Enjoy suggests pleasure. Your children should take pleasure in God as they continue knowing Him. It should not be a burden. So, education in and with Him should not be a burden, either.

Your children may not make it into Harvard or they may not be on the top of the bell curve. Your consolation is they will know God. What a consolation that is!

PHILOSOPHY & GOALS

In order to meet the goal of wisdom, virtue, and enjoying God in your young leaders, I suggest you take a look at your own philosophy of education. Take some time to see if your philosophy of education matches God's view of education. As you do so, you will begin to build your education paradigm.

How do **you** look at education? Do you believe educators need textbooks for everything? If so, you should realize that you are training your children to follow. The underlying assumption of textbooks is that you don't know enough to evaluate resources, so the textbook author will do it for you. To be educated, all the student has to do is learn the conclusions of the teacher. This model of education makes great followers who learn *what to think*.

Ponder for a moment. Textbooks give students questions to answer. If the student can answer the chosen questions on a test, he can move on to the next piece of information. Textbooks do not encourage students to think outside of the answers in the teacher's manual. This provides our society with highly trained, but poorly educated graduates.

I remember when Ashley had a fourth grade assignment to explain why George Washington was a Christian. She was attending a private school. When she looked at the information she was given, she wrote a paragraph saying she did not know if Washington was a Christian. Her teacher gave it back to her and asked her to re-do it. She wrote a similar answer because her photo and paragraph did not say anything about Washington trusting Christ as his Savior. The teacher returned her paragraph once again. Finally, I told Ashley to write the answer the teacher wanted, the answer included in the textbook teacher manual. She did so and received a high mark.

What an excellent example of a textbook and teacher only looking for one answer, the right one according to the teacher manual. How sad to think by fourth grade children were becoming followers of textbooks, even Christian textbooks like Ashley had. Ashley used critical and Biblical thinking skills for her assignment. The textbook drew the wrong conclusion that Washington was a Christian because he bought pews and served in the church. Many people give money and serve at church, but are not Christians. They have not seen their sin or trusted in Jesus death on the cross for the payment of their sin.

Ashley knew what a Christian was. She thought outside the box (or textbook). She was wrong in the factory school. She needed to mimic others, even if it was the wrong answer. She was pulled out of school that year so we could homeschool. We wanted more for our kids, so we pursued homeschooling to raise our children with a Biblical worldview.

APPROACHES TO CHRISTIAN HOMESCHOOLING

Besides the textbook model, what are other approaches to Christian homeschooling? Although these may be familiar to you, you may not have thought what the end result of using these approaches might be. Remember that "without a vision all the talk about reforming 'curriculum' will lead nowhere…for the question will always reemerge, "To what end? Why are we doing these things?" (John Gatto, *A Different Kind of Teacher)*. Keep your homeschooling vision and personal goals for your children close to heart as you choose an approach for your homeschool.

Although there are books written on each of these approaches individually, I will share in a nutshell the main idea as it relates to leadership education. If you would like to know more about each model described below, I recommend my book, *Approaches to Christian Homeschooling*.

Charlotte Mason is a leader in the homeschool movement of today. Her approach to education begins with solid character training. Character is also foundational in the leadership model. Followers of Charlotte Mason strive to develop an interest in learning, as well as a lifelong love of learning. To encourage a love of learning, Charlotte Mason homeschoolers read countless living books. Living books

> *Charlotte Mason:*
> *– Character*
> *– Love of Learning*
> *– Living Books*

have real-life ideas that families can discuss to promote critical and Biblical thinking. They can provide the basis for educating leaders since they can be a springboard for all types of discussion. Discussions provide opportunities for your children to practice thinking as you ask questions about the books.

Another homeschooling method is the classical approach which has recently become prominent in homeschool circles. One of the main goals of classical education is to teach your children *how to think*. When homeschoolers interact with their students in the same way Socrates and Plato interacted with their students, they begin providing an education for future leaders. Socrates and Plato discussed great ideas of their time. In a similar man-

> *Classical Education:*
> *– How to Think*
> *– Independent Study*

ner, you should discuss great ideas of our time. A word of caution, though. Many materials labeled classical do not truly help students learn how to think. They still follow a textbook mentality of telling students what to think. So, be careful to analyze curricula thoroughly before choosing it as a classical resource.

Independent study is another goal of classical education. This does not mean you choose programs that allow your student to work independently, like filling out a workbook independently. Independent studies should be based on a mentoring relationship. Socrates and Plato were mentors to their students. Follow their classical methods and you will develop leaders in your own students.

Unit studies allow you to relate your child's areas of learning to the real world and your family's interests. Taking a chosen topic and making it part of "real life" encourages students to see how learning should be a part of your life forever. Learning is life, itself. Therefore, unit studies encourage life-long learners. You may recall that life-long learning is a characteristic of leaders.

The next education model is the principle approach, which analyzes a given topic with Biblical principles. Whatever you are studying should be analyzed from a Biblical worldview. Applying Biblical principles to a variety of subject areas enlightens students in the way they should study for the rest of their lives. God is lord over the entire world and all areas of study. Thus, the principle approach ties together all areas of life with Biblical principles.

Unschooling is a method of education that allows the child to make all decisions about his own education. If he wants to study, great; if he doesn't want to study, he doesn't have to study. Taken to the extreme, this model is unbiblical. Proverbs 29:15 says, "*A* child left to himself brings shame to his mother". Some of you might think I'm arguing over semantics, but if you leave a child to do whatever he wants, you are not following the Bible. A child left to do as he pleases brings shame to his parents. God does not expect parents to allow their children to be the center of the family or the homeschool. Once again, taking this education model in its literal sense is not Biblical.

However, you can redefine unschooling to follow the grid of Scripture and offer benefits to your students. A family that provides a resource-rich environment from which their children can learn gives an alternative way of unschooling. When a child is surrounded by excellent learning resources, you encourage your children to love learning. As you provide a multitude of resources, you can allow them freedom to study their own chosen topics. This develops freedom, ownership and leadership skills in your children as they make their own choices. It also encourages them in making wise decisions with guidance from their parents.

COMBINE MODELS TO RAISE LEADERS

Leadership education uses a combination of these models, with some specific methods to achieve your end goal – know, glorify and enjoy God. As I explained each model of education above, you should see ways that leadership education is part of all of these approaches to homeschooling. These approaches will be mentioned throughout the rest of this book.

One of the essential elements of leadership education is teaching *how* to think. Above all else, your children should complete their education knowing *how* to think. Shifting your educational model from "what to think" to "how to think" can be a major change in your life. In order to set a foundation for this type of education, you need to start with yourself.

As you teach your children how to think, you might see lifestyle changes for your entire family. Leadership education ultimately involves the whole family. Initially, it takes much effort from a parent because you must be involved in learning and growing yourself. You cannot hand over workbooks and say "go for it". Workbooks merely teach your children *what* to think, not *how* to think. Your example of learning and growing begins the foundation of leadership education in your homeschool. Will you start today to be an example for your kids?

Additionally, you need to be excited about what you are learning in your own studies. Recently, I've been excited about what I'm reading. Even though my kids are out of the house, I still share what I'm learning. I'm excited about it; I file it quickly by journaling; I share it with my kids. As your children see their parents studying and learning, they begin to have a different idea of what education is all about. They have the opportunity to get excited about education.

GOALS FOR YOUR CHILD'S EDUCATION

The next step in changing your own education paradigm is letting go of the structured curriculum. If you really want to get off the conveyor belt of education and leave the factory school, let go of the structured curriculum and begin choosing what is best for your children. Consider the list you wrote

earlier about being successful in your child's education.
If you still haven't written
down your idea of successful
education, do that now.

It is not about the pro-
gram and finishing it each
year. Leadership education is
instilling a love of learning,

> *The priorities of our
> curriculum are daydreaming,
> natural and social sciences,
> self-discipline, respect of self
> and other, and making mistakes*
> *~ Mary Foley*

an ability to make wise decisions and thinking outside the box. Structured
curriculum teaches just the opposite. They train your children to follow
and think like their teacher. Leadership education allows students to think
for themselves and begin leading others.

From your list about education, it's time to list the goals for your children.
Contemplate for a moment what kind of goals you have for each child. You
probably have many academic goals. I realize that some of you are in states
where you must fulfill specific academic goals. You can line up your own
goals with the state's requirements through creativity. Creativity requires you
to think outside the box so this is a great example of using your skills of *how*
to think. Look at Mary Foley and her response to the local superintendent.

> *"If we are not free to educate our children, our liberty
> is an illusion. I do not have a curriculum. I have never
> used one... The state does not have the power to standard-
> ize children. My education philosophy precludes the use
> of a curriculum. My method has been successful enough
> to produce a daughter who is a member of the National
> Honor Society and twin sons who...tested in the top one
> percent on a national placement test for two consecutive
> years. The priorities of our curriculum are daydreaming,
> natural and social sciences, self-discipline, respect of self
> and other, and making mistakes."*
> **(Mary Foley, Homeschooling mother of four in Cape
> Cod, A Different Teacher)**

Too often, you become caught up in academic goals and forget your personal goals in character, in teaching your children to work, or in having a work ethic. You forget about your goals of maturing your children in Jesus Christ. You are so caught up in their studies and their schoolwork that you forget more important goals, in my opinion.

> *Finally, my brethren, whatever things are true, whatever things are noble, whatever things are just, whatever things are pure, whatever things are lovely, whatever things are of good report, if there is any virtue and if there is anything praiseworthy - meditate on these things.*
>
> **Philippians 4:8**

Use this verse as a goal and standard of what you study and how you spend your time. Then, you will cultivate wisdom, virtue and godly leaders of tomorrow.

But what about the basics? There are definitely basics your children need to survive in this world – reading, writing and simple calculations. Beyond this, you must decide your family's priorities. You may not cover the exact same materials as another family. That is okay!

Don't get worried about it…and don't worry if your family's goals don't line up with specific details of the public school, the factory with a conveyor belt. Get off the conveyor belt and do what is best for your own children. You are accountable to God for the way you raise your children. Look at the goals that God placed on your heart and fulfill those in rearing your children.

But you may not teach your children every detail of every subject that you studied growing up. Is that a problem? I don't think so.

GAPS IN EDUCATION

There are always gaps when it comes to education. Get used to the idea that your children will have gaps in their education. It's not a huge problem, if you choose carefully. What you must decide is what kinds of gaps you are willing to have in your children's education.

> *Will you have ...*
> *... Gaps in academics?*
> *... Gaps in character?*
> *... Gaps in your work ethic?*
> *... Gaps in Biblical training?*

In answering these questions, refer back to your priorities and make sure there aren't any gaps in your top priorities. For me, academics are further down the list. That does not mean my children will not be able to read, write, calculate solutions or study history.

However, they will initially develop a Biblical worldview so they can study other subject areas. My children will have Biblical training in Scripture in which to sift their lessons, to sift their books, so that they can make wise decisions in life. I am not willing to have a gap in my children's Biblical training, so I list that as a major goal in our children's education. I do not want gaps in their Biblical training. Although I don't want any gaps, I could live with gaps in other areas. You must decide which gaps you are willing to have and which gaps you are not willing to have. That's a decision only you and your spouse can make.

Keep your list of goals in front of you as you make decisions about your homeschool, especially at the beginning of each year. Pray about your list of goals - what God would have you do. Then, be sure your priorities are being fulfilled as you educate your children. Do not let others' opinions (even Grandma's) sway you from your goals and priorities.

HOW TO CHANGE YOUR OWN EDUCATION PARADIGM

As you re-think your education paradigm, I'd encourage you to begin your own educational journey. I can hear some of you right now.

"Well, I've already been to school. I graduated from high school. I went to college. Why do I have to start my own education?"

Why not take a step back and think about what we've said about leaders. Leaders are life-long learners. If you want to provide a leadership education for your child, you should model life-long learning yourself. If you're not interested in life-long learning for yourself, you might reconsider leadership education for your children.

How do your kids perceive education as they look at you? If you are not interested in your own education, why should your children be interested in their own education? If you believe graduating from high school or college is equal to an education, expect your children to believe the same. If you plan to mentor your children as future leaders, consider how you model learning in your family. Below is a personal growth plan centered on the classics. It's the same model I used when I began my educational journey as a homeschool mom.

READING CLASSICS

To begin your education, start with this short activity. It takes about a month. It's a great summer activity, but can be done any time of the year. Choose a classic to read the first week. If you're not sure what classic to read, there are some suggestions in my book, *Hop Off the Conveyor Belt.*

When I followed this simple plan, I began with *Little Britches.* You may think, "Well, that's not the *Iliad.* It's not Aristotle." When you start improving your education, I do not suggest plunging into difficult classics. Begin by reading a classic that captivates your attention and has endured over time. I know the *Iliad* has endured over time, but I don't think it's an appropriate book to begin your educational journey. Start with simpler books so that you understand the process of reading a classic each week. In the beginning, read for enjoyment.

The next step is: read another classic the following week. The next step is to read another classic. And then, read another classic. Now you've read four classics—mostly for enjoyment. After completing your last book, take a look at your book list. Jot down any ideas from these books, any lessons you've learned from the books and lessons you could teach your children. The main goal is to become involved in reading the classics, as well as making the classics a habit in your life.

At the time of this writing, I am reading *Pride and Prejudice,* by Jane Austen, again!! It is truly a classic that needs to be read several times. According to Italo Cavino, "A classic is a book that has never finished saying what it has to say".

> *A classic is a book that has never finished saying what it has to say*
>
> ~ *Italo Cavino*

When you read the next classic book (the fifth one), begin keeping a daily reading journal as you read. For each journal entry, write a simple summary of the section you read. You might include lessons you learn from that particular book or thoughts about the characters and plot. As I re-read *Pride and Prejudice,* I am struck by comments I did not catch the last time I read this book. Once you finish reading the classic, try to summarize five ideas from the book. Share those ideas with someone else.

You've just finished the parts of a personal growth plan as described earlier in this book. Set aside time to read. File quickly what you learn. Apply what you learned.

In the beginning, it's more about you, not them. First, you need to get started on your own education. You need to set aside time (read a classic), file quickly (reading journal) & apply (share). Begin with your own education.

Don't fall into the temptation of starting with your children until you've read at least five classics and kept a reading journal for at least one of those books. Once you finish your fifth classic book, you can get your children involved.

READING CLASSICS WITH YOUR CHILD

Actually, it's simple to change the structure of whatever you're doing right now to follow leadership education in your homeschool. The first thing to do with your children is choose a classic that you will read aloud together. Keep doing all the rest of the academic activities in your other subject areas. Make slow, gradual changes.

I recommend reading this first book aloud to model the entire process with your kids. When choosing a book to read, try and see what your children are interested in reading. Sometimes it is hard to get a consensus. If you have more than one child, let them take turns choosing the classics so you eventually read a book that everyone enjoys.

What if they choose a classic that you already read as a child? You need to re-read the classic. I read *Pride and Prejudice* in the past, so what? If you read it in years past, do you think you'll remember it all. I'm sure not.

> *No book that will not improve by repeated readings deserves to be read at all.*
> **Thomas Carlyle (1795-1881)**

Several years ago, Gentry read *A Tale of Two Cities* for a humanities class. I thought I'd use the "Cliff Notes". *A Tale of Two Cities* was one of my favorites in high school. Surely, I'll remember it well. I soon discovered a great dilemma: how horrible the discussions are when you haven't read a book in years. Now I read all the books that we discuss together, even if I read it in high school. If a book is classic, it is worth reading over and over and over again.

One of my goals as a homeschool mom is to read the books my kids are reading. Even if I've already read it, I will read it again. I know you can't keep up if you have more than a few children and you're trying to read six different books. It is impossible! To help you in this area, choose one book for all the children. Or divide your kids into two groups. Read one book with the older ones; read another book with the younger ones.

If it still seems overwhelming, then read your first classic out loud to everyone. They can simply listen to this classic as it is read aloud. If you feel led, discuss an event or circumstance each day. Or, wait until dinner and discuss it with Dad. In this way everyone listens to the same book and can discuss it together.

READING JOURNAL

The first time your family reads a classic, your priority should be reading for enjoyment. After reading a few classics with your children, aloud or individually, introduce the concept of a reading journal. Each child should have his own reading journal.

To make this extra special, I let each child choose a special notebook or binder to keep their reading journal entries. Some years, we would go to the store and let each child choose their reading journal. Have your child write a paragraph or two after reading each day. You should also keep your own notes as you read through these classics. Finally, once a week discuss the books with your children.

The discussion does not need to be formal. A discussion should be somewhat relaxed. I remember one year sitting in the bedroom with both of my daughters on the bed. We were discussing a book they were reading for an online class. I believe it was Dante's *Inferno*, not a simple book to assimilate. I was going through parts of that book and discussing it with them. Believe it or not, we were laughing some of the time. I'm sure you can imagine – two girls being silly about some comment that was made.

This is a great time to bond with your children, as well as a great time to bring up issues for discussion. And it can be relaxed! I know because we tend to be a relaxed family with our education.

Please note, I do not encourage you to start with Dante, nor would I encourage you to start with *The Iliad* or *The Odyssey* or Aristotle or Aquinas or any of the big names. Start with something your children will enjoy so they will be interested. You want to inspire them. Even choose something that's below their reading level at first.

That's what I did with my son one year. When we started choosing books for him to read that year, I purposely let him choose books below his reading level. You may wonder, why in the world did you do that? Or, you may think I should stretch him so he receives an excellent education.

I had another goal with my son that year. I strongly desired to bring him back to a point where he enjoyed reading books. He had grown tired of reading. He didn't enjoy it, so that year I took a different tack. I decided to let him make some choices, take ownership of his readings. He didn't have to read everything that mom chose and he didn't have to struggle to finish reading a book. I even found him reading on his bed at odd times during the day. I could see my goal being achieved. I believed this goal was important for Hunter, not what others said I should do this year. Thinking outside the box of curriculum is not always easy, but it sure can be profitable for your child.

SOCRATIC DISCUSSIONS

The next aspect of teaching your children *how to think* is having a Socratic discussion, either with your children or as a group with other students.

> *Never answer your own question!*

One way to structure your time as a group is to choose a classic that everyone will read, as you've already done. Throughout the week each group or family member keeps a reading journal about the chosen book. Plan a time to meet together, once a week and gather for discussion.

When you meet together, choose one of the adults to guide the discussion. Use open-ended questions to generate more than "yes-no" answers. Be sure not to answer your own questions. Yes, waiting for answers is extremely difficult.

If it's quiet, so what? Quiet time gives your students time to think. If you are always jumping in, trying to give answers, you never give your children time to think or a chance to learn how to think. They learn quickly that mom will answer her own questions so they do not need to think very hard.

To me, this is one of the drawbacks of grade-level schools. There is a sense that a teacher must cover many subjects in a certain number of minutes. In doing so, she does not give students a chance to think and answer their own questions. Generally speaking, teachers force-feed information to their students because it's more efficient. However, it is not more educational.

As I recall my years as a public school teacher, I am reminded of one particular workshop that improved my teaching style. I taught fifth grade for six years. During one of my last years, I attended a summer workshop on teaching the Junior Great Books with the Socratic method. At the time, I did not have the big picture of classics and discussions. But I did learn one valuable lesson. When I ask students a question, give them time to think of an answer.

If you've given them a long time to think (at least two solid minutes of peace and quiet), still keep your answer to yourself. Pose another question that will help your students come up with answers. Don't ever answer your own question! If you need to make a comment, make it the form of another question. Remember, you are the guide to the discussion. You are not the teacher; you are not the professor. You are a guide to the discussion so your children will learn how to think.

If you think this sounds totally impossible, I suggest getting a copy of *Teaching the Classics,* by Adam Andrews (listed in Resources). This guide is helpful if you feel a bit insecure in the Socratic method. Using the Socratic method, Mr. Andrews shows you how to analyze the classics, how to look at the plot structure, and how to look at the characters, setting and themes.

One of my favorite aspects of *Teaching the Classics* is the way it starts with very simple children's books. The first one is *Peter Rabbit*. Socratic discussions should begin with very young children to give them a chance of learning how to think, even with *Peter Rabbit*. Use simple story books to teach plot and character. If you have children that are twelve years old, start with simple story books to help them understand the different elements of a book. Since it is very easy to understand a story book, students can take those ideas and apply it to classics on their reading level. By the way, did you know *Peter Rabbit* is a classic. It's been around for decades and has endured the test of time.

Start with Yourself
Read Classics
Reading Journal
Socratic Discussions

To recap, here is a simple plan to start your own personal growth plan and begin learning "how to think". Start with yourself, reading classics and keeping your own reading journal. Once you gain success with a few classics yourself, then move on to your children. Encourage them as they read classics and have discussions as a family. It sounds quite easy. Actually it isn't that hard to do when you take it one simple step at a time.

CHARACTER IS FOUNDATIONAL

INTRODUCTION TO CHARACTER

The rest of this book will deal with age-appropriate methods to raise leaders, starting with character development and moving to inspiring a love of learning. After your children have a foundation in character and a love for learning, they move to independent studies with a mentor. The ideas here are incremental in nature. Even if you have an older child, you must be sure they have the foundation to study independently. If you expect a fifteen year old to study independently, without strong character or a desire to learn, you will have problems at home. Lay the foundation first. Then, move on to independent studies and mentors.

Why approach education this way, developing character and inspiring our children to learn? The answer is to develop leaders who have the tools to research given subjects and the character to make wise decisions.

START "OFF" THE CONVEYOR BELT

Character is essential, no matter what age. Many people ask me when they should start educating for leadership. Do you wait until your children are old enough for independent studies? No! Start as early as possible. The earlier you start your children to learn "off the conveyor belt", the better for you and your children.

Can you imagine what it would be like to grow up without the drudgery of "school"? I think it would be grand to not have baggage from the factory

The earlier you start your children to learn "off the conveyor belt", the better

school or conveyor belt. Start your children with a proper view of education to avoid a "hate of learning", like the conveyor belt students. When you offer an alternative to the conveyor belt, your children realize that school is not the only place you learn. You can learn anywhere and everywhere.

Since I did not start my children with an optimistic view of education, I spent time re-adjusting our attitude about education. At times I tell my children, "It's just life. We're doing life". They think I'm a little crazy. When they think of school, they think of "to do" lists for education. Your children may want you telling them what to do so they can finish and go play. Changing this attitude takes time and diligence on your part, the parent. If you do not want your children to have this attitude, plan to spend time doing activities that are educational, but not schoolish.

I want my children to have an attitude of lifelong learning and a desire to learn for the rest of their life. If I could start over, I'd begin at a very young age, encouraging a love of learning with strong character along the way. My two-year old granddaughter loves to "read". She turns the pages and tells the story to her doll who sits in the chair next to her. Why does she do this at two years of age? Her dad and mom read to her each and every day. She already loves books. Kids at this age are naturally curious and love learning. Even two-year olds can start to love learning.

Another aspect of changing your family's view of education is the area of character development. Like I said earlier, character is foundational when it comes to leadership education. If you start your children early in developing their character, you're starting off on the right foot.

You can't really proceed with education unless a student has strong character development. If your child does not have a foundation in solid character, that's where you need to start. Even if your child is thirteen or older, start with character if they lack character development. If your child does not exhibit integrity, courage and perseverance, it is unlikely he will work well on his own. I encourage you to take a month or two to work on character development and the work ethic. Your child needs to develop both of these areas so he can work independently and prepare to be a godly leader.

CLOSE ANY CHARACTER GAPS

While you develop character in your children, be sure to look for "gaps" to close. Character training and Biblical training are the two places that I refuse to leave gaps. I realize there will be gaps in my children's upbringing because I'm imperfect. I can't do everything right. But I will strive to close the gaps in

> *Character training and Biblical training are the two places that I refuse to leave gaps.*

these two areas, above everything. If your child has integrity, ingenuity, humility, courage, work ethic, perseverance, he will make it in life. Your child may not understand all the details of Trigonometry, but with the ability to persevere he can be a successful leader.

When your children are young, ninety percent of their education should be in character. Use those years to develop compassion, kindness, ingenuity, integrity, humility and perseverance, to name a few qualities. Provide opportunities for your children to fail and succeed. We learn more from our failures than our successes, so use those mistakes to teach and mature your children. Is it okay if they fail? Of course it is, if you use the failure as a teaching opportunity.

Too often we want to force academics at a young of an age. We want to keep up with facebook, pinterest and Instagram. And then what happens? Just like the story at the beginning of the book, children who go to kindergarten where academics are pushed down their throat. They don't like school anymore, nor do they enjoy any type of learning. What has actually been taught to these children is a dislike academics. Watch the amount of time you spend on academics with children under ten years of age so you give them the best chance to love learning. Early academics does not provide a solid education.

KEEP THE WAYS OF THE LORD

*For I have known him (Abraham), in order that he may com-
mand his children and his household after him, that they keep
the way of the Lord, to do righteousness and justice, that the
Lord may bring to Abraham what He has spoken to him.*

Genesis 18:19

What a great goal for parents today! Let's look at these verses in detail. You command your children. That sounds a bit harsh by today's standards, but it simply means the father is head of his household. Fathers should have children that obey him. Obviously, this implies you interact with your children.

Not only is there a fear of Dad, but there is a love of Dad to obey. The result of having children who obey is they *keep the way of the Lord*. One of your primary goals in child-raising is for your children to follow in the ways of the Lord…for the rest of their lives.

Pray daily that your children will grow up, get married, have their own families, all the time walking in the ways of the Lord. This has been one of my prayers for our children since they were young. I still pray for my children to follow God in all they do and to marry a strong believer who will encourage them in godliness. Sure, I pray for them to do well at their basketball game or to get well. But, the most important prayer I can offer for them is to walk closely with their God.

*He has shown you, O man, what is good;
And what does the Lord require of you
But to do justly,
To love mercy,
And to walk humbly with your God*

Micah 6:8

Spend time teaching your children what justice, mercy and humility is so they can walk in those ways forever. Then, fall on your knees and ask God that His Holy Spirit will empower your children to walk uprightly with Him the rest of their lives.

CHARACTER QUALITIES

Whathat character qualities should you develop in your children so they will grow up to be leaders? One of the central qualities I believe a leader must have is a good attitude. I don't want to endorse the positive thinking movement. However, it is important to instill a positive attitude in your children. The attitude of "I can" is half the battle when working through issues. Why not memorize this verse with your family?

> *I can do all things through Christ who strengthens me.*
> ***Philippians 4:13***

When you have a negative, or "I might", attitude you start one step behind everyone else. Most people, adults and children, with a negative attitude are usually afraid of failure. Leaders are not afraid of risk or failure. As a leader, you may not like failure, but you understand the value of learning from your mistakes. Those with a negative attitude also make multitudes of excuses of why they can't be successful. If you see your kids giving you lots of excuses, spend time helping them understand that with Christ they can do all things.

I read a story about a one-arm golfer with a near-perfect stroke. Onlookers were amazed because those with two arms couldn't do nearly as well. The golfer said, "It's my experience that the right attitude and one arm will beat the wrong attitude and two arms every time." Not only does this hold true for the golf course, but in all facets of life. Teach your children the importance of a right attitude.

> *But the fruit of the Spirit is love, joy, peace, longsuffering, kindness, goodness, faithfulness, gentleness, self-control. Against such there is no law.*
> **Galatians 5:22-23**

Let's get down to specific character qualities. I encourage parents to start with the fruit of the Spirit which offers a general list of godly character. Remember all fruit is inspired by the Holy Spirit, who develops these qualities in your children's lives. You are His instrument to teach your children.

HUMILITY VS PRIDE

Submission and humility are essential to be a godly leader. That may sound counter-intuitive to being a leader. Our culture looks down on humility, but a true leader is humble. I'm not a big fan of Confucius but he offers much insight when he says, "Humility is the solid foundation of all virtues." One of our goals in

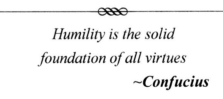

Humility is the solid foundation of all virtues
~Confucius

leadership education is to cultivate wisdom and virtue. Humility is the best place to start in cultivating virtue. Early church leader, Saint Augustine, begins with humility to build something great.

> *Do you wish to rise? Begin by descending. You plan a tower that will pierce the clouds? Lay first the foundation of humility.*
> *~Saint Augustine*

I believe strong leaders are humble, by admitting their mistakes and taking advice from others. If you have a problem with pride, other problems will continually arise in your life. God despises pride and weeds it out of His own children, both adults and children.

> *Pride goes before destruction and a haughty spirit before a fall. Better to be of a humble spirit with the lowly than to divide the spoil with the proud.*
>
> **Proverbs 16:18**

> *These six things the Lord hates, yes, seven are an abomination to Him: a proud look...*
>
> **Proverbs 6:16-17**

The very first thing God mentions that He hates abominably is pride. Pride is the beginning of most falls in life. When you are proud, eventually you will fall. So, teach your children the pitfalls of pride and the benefits of humility.

God seeks humility in His children. In James 4:6, we read that "God resists the proud, but gives grace to the humble". Humility is definitely a Biblical concept that God honors.

> *Let nothing be done through selfish ambition or conceit, but in lowliness of mind let each esteem others better than himself. Let each of you look out not only for his own interests, but also for the interests of others. Let this mind be in you which was also in Christ Jesus.*
>
> **Philippians 2:3-5**

Jesus Christ is the ultimate example. After Paul's comments above, he uses Christ as the greatest example of humility, leaving heaven to become a bondservant on earth. Not only was Christ a bondservant, He humbled Himself to the point of death on the cross. Christ exemplifies the extreme in humility; he also exemplifies the extreme in exaltation. God the Father exalts Jesus Christ above every name given. All mankind will bow and worship Jesus as Christ and Lord. Humility and exaltation appear as an oxymoron, but not in God's eyes. God honors Christ's humility and exalts Him above all. God will honor humility in your family, as well.

Use Jesus Christ as an example to teach your children the importance of humility. Your children should have this Biblical view of humility so they can lead America back to its Biblical roots. As they change society, your children should lead and evaluate issues with Scripture as their guide.

Begin by memorizing verses as a family. You might choose some of the verses mentioned in this chapter. Next, read some Bible stories illustrating humility or pride. A few that come to mind are below.

Nebuchadnezzar – Daniel 4:30-34, 5:20 (pride, ate grass like oxen)
Haman – Esther 5:11, 6-7 (pride, brought low)
Joseph – Genesis 41 (humility in prison, given understanding, ruler)
Ruth – Ruth 2, 4 (humility serving mother-in-law, in lineage of Christ)

Next, set up opportunities in your home for your children to learn humility. It usually doesn't take much, except human natures, to set up an opportunity to be humble. When my children were young, and even now as they are older, there are many chances for them to be humble and think more of their siblings than themselves.

A hands-on activity to root out pride from your children is making the proud child serve a sibling. You can reward the humble child by letting him become the master of the proud child. For a short time, the proud child must serve another. The proud child needs to do what the humble child says, since he is the temporary master. By serving a sibling, your proud child should learn the importance of humility.

COURAGE & INTEGRITY

Courage and integrity should be taught at a young age. Your children should have the ability to stand up for what is right and godly. This is difficult enough as adults, much less for your children. I know from my own experience, it is difficult to go against the crowd and do what God says is right.

> *And do not be conformed to this world, but be transformed by the renewing of your mind, that you may prove what is that good and acceptable and perfect will of God.*
>
> **Romans 12:2**

Yet, from an early age you should teach your children what is right and wrong. Encourage your young ones to do what is right on a regular basis so it will become a habit in their lives. As they grow up, they'll have plenty of chances to take a stand for the right decision.

TRUTHFULNESS

Truthfulness is important to teach your children in this day and age because many Americans think it is okay to lie. We live in a Machiavellian world where the end justifies the means. It doesn't matter what you say or do, as long as you get the result that you need.

> *...putting away lying, "Let each one of you speak truth with his neighbor," for we are members of one another.*
>
> **Ephesians 4:25**

According to the Scriptures your truthfulness, or lack thereof, affects those around you. We are members of one another and our actions influence our home, church and community. From a very young age, your children are tempted to lie in order to avoid consequences.

My children received automatic spankings for two actions: disrespecting their mother and lying. Lying was a serious offense in our home and it still is. Take your time and always discipline for lying. Sometimes your children's lies are funny or cute. Do not let them win and avoid punishment for lying.

*Your tongue devises destruction, Like a sharp razor, work-
ing deceitfully. You love evil more than good, Lying rather
than speaking righteousness.*

Psalms 52:2-3

If you'd like to show your child the seriousness of lying, read the verses
above. Then, pull out a razor and discuss what a razor can do, the potential
for pain, violence and destruction. Explain that lying is the same; it has
the potential to cause pain, violence and destruction to their family and
friends.

*Righteous lips are the delight of kings, And they love him
who speaks what is right.*

Proverbs 16:13

As you teach the destruction of lying, be sure to show your kids the benefits of being honest. When your child is honest, treat him special. Explain
that kings love honesty, so you're going to do something special for him
or her. This might include a special outing, choosing what's for dinner, a
special gift or a special privilege. It's up to you (the king of your family)
to decide how you will honor honesty.

PERSEVERANCE & WORK ETHIC

The last qualities on my list, but certainly not the last character qualities to
ever develop, are perseverance and work ethic. It is important as leaders to
complete tasks and projects. Tasks may be simple activities, like making
your bed or emptying the dishwasher. Projects are bigger activities, like
planning a birthday party or cleaning the garage. Projects are a combination of many little tasks. In order to complete tasks and projects, you must
have a positive work ethic.

Should you reward your kids for a job well done? I could write another
book on this topic and all the opinions for parents. Personally, I believe
rewards are Scriptural and appropriate in certain situations.

I remember when I was potty training one of my children. I asked older moms to find out the best method for success. All the moms told me they eventually used some sort of reward. Thus, I decided to start with the reward system because I wanted to be finished with potty training as soon as possible. I began by giving a small piece of candy each time they were successful. Some Christians believe rewards are a superficial means to an end. If you have this attitude and are still unsure about using rewards, go to the Scriptures. Do a word study on rewards and you will have a more complete picture of God's view of rewards. Plus, you might come away with a different perspective on rewarding your children.

Do I still give my children rewards for jobs around the house? No! As my children have grown up, I quit giving them candy or a sticker for every little thing they do. I don't even give them a big reward. When it's cleaning day, we all have our tasks, whether it's cleaning a bathroom or vacuuming. We all pitch in together to get the house clean. There's no reward now, that's just part of living in our house and working hard to get the house clean.

Sometimes, rewards are appropriate and other times they are not. This is where wisdom from God is used. I've used rewards for some tasks and not for others. I recommend prayerfully considering when to reward your kids and when not to reward.

TEACHING THE WORK ETHIC

Eventually you will move away from the reward and teach your children the importance of working hard. Include Scripture as you teach them the concept of working hard. One way to impress the work ethic upon your children is to study Proverbs 6:6-11 and learn from our friend, the ant.

> *Go to the ant, you sluggard, consider her ways and be wise.*
> *Which having to no captain, overseer, or ruler provides her*
> *supplies in the summer and gathers her food in the harvest.*
> *How long will you slumber, oh sluggard? When will you*
> *rise from your sleep? A little sleep, a little slumber, a little*

*folding of the hands to sleep, so shall you poverty come on
you like a prowler and your need like an armed man.*
Proverbs 6:6-11

There are so many concepts about work ethic in those few verses. You could use that one paragraph for daily devotions for a week or once a week for a month. Talk to your children about the rewards of hard work and the consequences of being a lazy person - the old sluggard that doesn't do anything. You might buy an anthill project to watch and see what ants are like. Ants provide a picture of hard work. Most kids learn from projects like ant farms, especially when you can learn in an informal way.

Another tool in helping your children see the importance of work is a chart called *Go To The Ant Chart*. This chart goes on your refrigerator and organizes ways to teach work ethic and perseverance. You will find links to this chart in the Resources section.

Developing a solid work ethic is the basis for being an entrepreneur in the future. Entrepreneurs are not afraid of hard work because they have a vision of what results from hard work.

True entrepreneurs are the business leaders, the movers and the shakers of local communities. Self-employed businessmen are not always entrepreneurs because they often live as a slave to their own business. Entrepreneurs are ones who step back and manage people, manage businesses and manage jobs. To do their job well, they need to do it with a good attitude. These are the men and women who will change society in the future because they aren't afraid of working hard.

MOTIVATIONS TO PERSEVERE

What motivates your children to work hard? Rewards can be given individually with sticker charts. Young children love stickers. When my kids were young, we had simple grids on the refrigerator for stickers. When a child obeyed or persevered, they were given a sticker. When the chart was full, we all got a treat. It might be going out for ice cream or going to the park.

Another system is filling a jar with marbles whenever a task is completed. Tasks may be chores around the house, completing studies or whatever you are teaching your children at the time. Each time a task is completed, you drop a marble in the jar. Once the jar is full, your family receives a reward.

At other times you need to motivate your children with punishment. There's nothing wrong with that.

> *Do not withhold correction from a child. For if you beat him with a rod, he will not die. You shall beat him with a rod and deliver his soul from Hell.*
>
> **Proverbs 23:13**

There is a time and a place for Biblical correction and punishment. Of course, this assumes you have a Biblical understanding of punishment, just like you should have a Biblical understanding of rewards. It is necessary to use God's wisdom to know what is appropriate with your own children. When you use correction and punishment, Proverbs says we deliver a soul from Hell. When we do not use correction, the opposite is true. Your child is not delivered from Hell or raised to God.

Another method of motivating your children to complete their work is competition. Competition between siblings is healthy and works well with some children. I remember a time when my mom wanted us to make our beds daily. She checked our room every morning to see who had made their bed and kept a record. At the end of the week, she rewarded the one who made his bed the most. That's just a simple way to use competition to do a good job.

For some kids, competition does not motivate. This child might be more motivated simply by the praise and reward of a parent. Most children yearn to please their parents. When you praise them for a job well done, it means more than you might realize. The opposite can also be true. Fear can be a good motivator, too. Usually children have a healthy fear of Dad which I think is fantastic. When Dad steps in after Mom's been home all day, children often think twice about what they are doing. Dad's simple instructions can motivate children to get his job done.

These are just a few ways to motivate children to work quickly, cheerfully and completely. Realize that your children are motivated by different things. You should watch and see what works best with each child. Your ultimate goal is for your children to work hard to please God.

The ultimate goal for my children's work is working heartily for the Lord, because their ultimate reward is with Him.

BETTER UNDERSTANDING OF GOD'S WORD

As your family grows up, I recommend getting a firm understanding of God's view of work. Have morning devotions about work once a week, discussing what God's idea of work is. Use Scripture to support your conclusions about work.

This is an excellent activity because you are modeling how to use a Biblical worldview with every day life. In your discussion of Scriptures, point out practical

> *Whatever you do, do it heartily*
> *as to the Lord and not to men,*
> *knowing that from the Lord*
> *you will receive the reward of*
> *the inheritance for you serve*
> *the Lord Christ.*
> **Colossians 3:23**

applications in your own home and family. Are you really pleasing to God in the way you work around your home? Be prepared: this may be convicting to parents, as well as children. God convicts me when I teach my kids.

TOOLS TO ENCOURAGE CHARACTER

The character qualities listed above are a place for you to start with your family. It is not extensive, but does offer some ideas for your family. Some of my favorite tools are listed below. Each one has a link to my review so you can decide if it will be a good fit for your family.

FOR INSTRUCTION IN RIGHTEOUSNESS

My favorite tool for character building is *For Instructions in Righteousness*, a great, big, wonderful manual. I bought this at my very first homeschool convention and used it every year thereafter.

For Instruction in Righteousness has Scriptures throughout that are categorized according to sins. That may seem odd, but bear with me. On the opposite side of the sin, you find a list of blessings for obedience. When you look up the sin of pride, you see verses dealing with pride, God's view of pride, punishment for pride, and so on. Next you will have verses that show the blessings of humility.

How did I use this manual? When my children were young, I chose a few verses to read and discuss. Many verses listed in *For Instruction in Righteousness* include suggested applications. I used those, as well.

I would read the verse to whichever child was the offender. We would discuss how to change behavior and any consequences for wrong behavior.

As my children grew up, they began to look up verses themselves. I handed them the manual. They had to look up at least three verses about that sin and write what they learned. If they were dealing with impatience, they chose verses to read and report to me. Then, we would discuss what should be done.

http://HowToHomeschoolMyChild.com/character-training

BIBLE CHARACTER CHARTS

The *If-Then Chart* is intended to help you be more consistent in your discipline. When your child disobeys, the chart helps you quickly know what to do from a Biblical perspective. Your child can see for himself what is expected after his action. The chart has three columns: the misbehavior, a corresponding verse, and a blank for you to write in an appropriate consequence. I recommend laminating the chart so you can change consequences to fit your seasons of life.

This is the fun one! The *Blessing Chart* is designed to help you acknowledge and reward godly attitudes and behavior. The left-hand column lists good character qualities, with cartoon drawings. The center column quotes Scripture verses that tell how God blesses us when these qualities are present in our lives. The right-hand column is left blank, for you to write in agreed-upon rewards.

The chart instructions give many ideas for creative rewards that relate to God's rewards in our lives. For example, under "peacemaking" one of the verses listed is Matthew 23:12, which says, "he who humbles himself will be exalted." The instructions offer ideas for ways to "exalt" your peacemaker: a party or feast with the family, no chores for a day, a "Servant's Day" when the family performs services for the "exalted" child, or flying a special name flag from your front porch.

The one thing that probably wears me down more than anything else as a mother is bickering: petty arguments and their results. "Maaah-meeee, he hit me!" I used to feel like a referee!

I began to see that I was also encouraging my children to become gossips as they constantly reported their grievances to me. We knew there had to be an answer! So we started digging into God's Word. *The Brother Offended Checklist* is in a format that even a toddler (or adult) can understand!

The *Go To The Ant Chart* arms you with Scripture to work with your easily distracted or "less than diligent" child. You will find every area of laziness imaginable, plus a Bible verse for each problem, an easy reference when they're driving you crazy! Take your child to the chart, identify his slothful action or attitude, read what God says about it, and pray for His strength to obey.

If you decide to get *For Instruction in Righteousness* and the four small charts listed above, check out our website for a special bundle price.

http://HowToHomeschoolMyChild.com/character-training

If you want to tie classics into character training, there are plenty of books you can read. One of our family favorites is the *Little Britches* series. Ralph Moody wrote about his own childhood during the early twentieth century. Your children will be enthralled with his portrayal of life at this time. You will be encouraged with how many opportunities you have for meaningful discussions. Moody provides real life stories that show ingenuity, integrity, humility, courage and perseverance. These books are excellent. Another book we all enjoyed is *Laddie*, a great book with many life lessons about family relationships and hard work.

GOD'S CALLING

As you encourage strong character in your children, begin to show them they have a calling from God to fulfill.

God has a purpose for each one of His children here on earth. Your children should learn their calling was set before creation.

> *I press toward the goal for the prize of the upward call of God in Christ Jesus.*
>
> **Philippians 3:14**

...that the God of our Lord Jesus Christ, the Father of glory, may give to you the spirit of wisdom and revelation in the knowledge of Him, the eyes of your understanding being enlightened; that you may know what is the hope of His calling, what are the riches of the glory of His inheritance in the saints.

Ephesians 1:17-18

Strive to know God's calling for you and your children. As you can see from the verses above, you must use wisdom and understanding to see the hope of God's calling for each person in your family.

In order to fulfill God's calling, your children need to mature in their godly character. If your children are following God, but don't have godly character, they eventually run into problems.

Too often we treat our young children like young adults, expecting them to sit in a chair and study. I think it's important that we treat them as children and allow them to fulfill God's calling for them, as a child. Part of His calling for children is to play and develop integrity, humility, perseverance. Get outside the box while you spend time teaching character to your young children.

> *...who has saved us and called us with a holy calling, not according to our works, but according to His own purpose and grace which was given to us in Christ Jesus before time began*
>
> **2 Timothy 1:9**

On the other hand, our society treats teenagers like they're children, expecting them to play and not assume responsibility. This goes against God's calling for teens. If you have teenagers, treat them as young adults. Give them real-life responsibilities to fulfill.

If you plan to educate your teenager by getting off the conveyor belt, begin slowly with small responsibilities. Getting off the conveyor belt will probably be a shock to your teens. Let them be successful with jobs around your home before you expect them to be responsible for their own education. Be sure you have consequences for not being responsible and enforce them consistently.

Many of you want to push, push, push academics at the expense of character. Please do not pursue academics without a solid foundation in your child's character. You'll be so glad you started with Godly character before moving towards academics,

LOVE OF
LEARNING

INTRODUCTION TO LOVE OF LEARNING

The next step in raising leaders, not followers, is giving your children a love of learning. Inspire and motivate them to learn on their own and you'll create life-long learners. Don't stop character training just because you're moving on to a new section of leadership education. Simply add "love of learning" activities to your homeschool.

Children who enjoy learning and discovery are those that truly have a love of learning. Children are naturally curious and want to learn about everything. But send them to school and you often squelch their enthusiasm. Worksheets, review books, and tests, as well as making them sit rigidly in a chair take away their natural curiosity. During this young age, focus on drawing out your children's natural love of learning at an early age so it continues through life.

Keep in mind that a love of learning begins with you. This is similar to the getting started ideas where you read classics before you introduce them to your children. If you personally do not have a love of learning, you need to establish your own love of learning first.

When your children see their own parents continually learning more, your excitement will promote a love of learning in your children. My own children tease me about how much I enjoy learning. I don't mind their teasing because they know how important learning is to me. As my children get older they are sensing their own excitement and desire to continue learning for a lifetime.

If your children have a "hate" of learning, you should strive to change their attitude before you introduce them to independent studies. Consider the reasons your child hates learning. Their hate of learning did not happen instantly. Change your daily routine and allow more freedom to study your children's interests. Use your child's interests as you choose books, create activities or have them write. Get excited yourself about your new discoveries. Eventually your enthusiasm will rub off. This will take time; it will not happen overnight.

FAMILY LIFESTYLE OF LEARNING

To develop a love of learning in your children, you may need to change your lifestyle to one of discovery and learning, not workbooks which give the appearance of learning. Think about this for a minute. When you want to learn something, do you get a workbook and fill it out? Maybe if you're figuring out finances you fill out a workbook. For the most part, you don't study a workbook to learn something. You go to the library, get books and read about your chosen topic. You discuss it with other people in your family so that it becomes a real life experience; it becomes part of you.

If you are learning and loving your education, it will transfer to your children. Several of my newsletter readers have asked me about this issue. Let me share about Ashley, who matured in her desire to learn, going beyond just a love of learning.

In high school, she chose classes she wanted to take in furthering her education. One was Greek and the other was Astronomy. These were her interests, not mine. We agreed to help her find somewhere she could learn about these topics. She found someone who could mentor her in these subject areas. For Greek she attended a class at the local college and for Astronomy she took an online class. After that semester, she furthered her own education by choosing other topics she wants to study, possibly shadowing someone and continuing her Greek class.

INSPIRE, NOT REQUIRE

If you want to develop a love of learning, there are two areas you need to address. One is to inspire, not require as DeMille suggests in *A Thomas Jefferson Education*. The other is to motivate your child. There's a lot of crossover in this information, but let's move on and see how you can inspire your children.

I love the idea of truly inspiring your children. Although I believe wholeheartedly with inspiring my own children, I am not perfect. Sometimes I fall back on the workbook learning. But my goal is to inspire my children to love learning and discovery. I want them to be leaders, not followers.

When they follow that workbook, they often jump back on that conveyor belt and become a follower who doesn't learn how to think. Initially, strive to inspire without textbooks or workbooks. Your children will be surprised at your new approach and that surprise might be enough to inspire them to learn more.

You will definitely have opposition from those around you if you take an inspiration approach to education. You will surely hear, "What about the basics?" My question to these doubters is, "What are the basics? Basics according to whom?" You are the parent and know your child better than anyone else. Don't forget that you are the expert on your child. You determine the basics for your family.

> *You are the expert on your child. You determine the basics for your family.*

From my own experience, I believe "basics" begin with Bible training and nothing else. From there, basics move to character development and maturity. What most people would call "school" comes after Bible training and character development in my home. I really don't like the word school because of all its connotations.

Earlier I told you I was a school teacher for six years. On top of that, my children attended a good, private, Christian school for several years.

During those years of conveyor belt school, I often felt like I was dropping them off at prison. They were stuck in that building all day long and it wasn't real life. My children learned how to memorize many facts, but they did not learn how to think. In my mind the word "school" does not inspire me to learn; it actually does just the opposite.

I tried to change our family's attitude about school by changing the name. Many times I used the term, "children's studies", instead of "schoolwork", to encourage a different attitude. When my children have a choice in their "studies", they are more likely to enjoy their daily time spent learning. Since my children went to school, it takes awhile to change their view of school. Getting off the conveyor belt can be just as hard for your children as it is for you.

Most of you think about schoolwork and homeschool as 'have-to's' instead of privileges. Consider changing your own attitude of a checklist mentality in order to change your children's view of school. Count it a privilege to learn. Encourage your children to understand what a privilege it is to read and write. Brainstorm together why learning is a privilege. This is so important!

It's a privilege for all of us to be able to communicate with others. It's a privilege to learn history. Why learn history? History repeats itself and you don't want to make the same mistakes as were made in the past. It's a privilege to learn math. Math relates to everyday life. Even algebra can be related to everyday life, whether your child believes it or not.

One of the best ways to inspire your children is giving them a reason why. When your kids ask why, what's your normal response? Because I said so! Sound familiar? I've been guilty of this, but it does not give your children a reason why. Excellent employers realize their employees do a better job when given the big picture. When the employee sees how their job fits in with the entire company, they take pride in their job and excel.

You need to remember that your school, or studies, should have a purpose beyond a list of

> *Give your child a "reason why"*

what every fourth grader should know. When your children understand why they must identify nouns, they are more encouraged to learn them.

Take some time and write a list of why your child is studying the subjects he has. Over the next few weeks, visit with your child about each subject area and why he is studying it. The reason why may look different for each family.

A RABBIT TRAIL

I realize the introduction to this section is "inspire, not require," but I must digress about things to require. You are the parent and you are accountable to God for raising your children. Thus, you have certain obligations to God to raise your children according to His Word. I believe those requirements center around the Bible, more than academics. For this reason, you should have household requirements. My children had to learn obedience while gaining a love of learning.

If you show your children the reason why you are requiring a particular task or activity, it makes follow-through a lot easier. Let's look at some of my family requirements. They may be different from your family requirements, but you will get the idea. First, we require some of the basics I

> *What are your family requirements?*

just mentioned, beginning with the Bible. Why? To rule and reign for Christ. Another basic requirement is character. Sounds like a broken record!! I think you've read this a few times because it is so important to me. Bible training and character development are basics that we often overlook at the expense of what we call, academics. Both are required in my homeschool.

Reading was required, so our children read everyday. When they were young, we had an hour of quiet time in their bedroom after lunch every day. This allowed each child to read silently for an hour. We tried to choose books the children enjoyed and coincided with topics we were studying.

I wanted my children to love books and not see reading as a chore. Trying to change my son's attitude about reading was my project that one year. Since he did not like reading, I quickly learned he should spend more time reading books of his interests. Hunter did read a history book, even though he could care less about history. Instead of making history such a chore to him, we read historical fiction aloud together and talked about it. His independent reading centered around his interests.

Our children are required to write and communicate. I try to tie their written papers with topics in which they have an interest. When your children are interested in a given topic, won't their writing be better? My kids' writing is always better when they could choose the topic. I am more focused on the writing skills than the topic they choose. Therefore, we bring reading and writing into areas of our children's interests.

History is an activity that we always do together as a family, first thing in the morning. Why? To learn the lessons of the past that we need to imitate or avoid.

Math is a subject in which I let my older daughters choose to complete. Are you surprised I let them choose to study Math? Neither one of my daughters enjoys math, so I don't think they are called to enter a mathematical field. They have a basic understanding of Math concepts, including Algebra. One of my daughters chose to continue Math through Algebra 2. She desires to attend a university and realizes she must have some math background to enter college. Even though she chooses to do math, she does not solely use a traditional book. She uses a math book and a supplemental CD that teaches each lesson from a Christian perspective. Why do we study math? So our children can survive in today's society. They should also understand mathematical concepts to teach their own children.

I listed my personal reasons for studying particular subjects. You must decide for your family why you study different topics. Is your reasoning just to get into college or obtain a job? If so, take some time and think of real life reasons why your family studies History, Math or Literature. Those are the reasons that will make a difference with your children.

FREEDOM TO CHOOSE

Believe it or not, you and your children still have freedom in your homeschool. Freedom in homeschooling is important because it allows you a chance to model freedom while your children are still at home. Remember that you are the expert on your child.

You should be free to make choices of when to study any given subject. Decide what and when you need to require specific studies. Contemplate if you should teach every subject every year. Why or why not? Do you study every subject, every year just because the schools do? Why are you following the conveyor belt model? Use God's wisdom to decide what is best for your own children.

At times, I desire to do just the opposite of the public schools. Since they use a conveyor belt mentality, I want to run in the opposite direction from their priorities and approaches. The conveyor belt is a failure when it comes to education, so why follow in their footsteps.

One example of their failure is the fact that many public schools today try to teach critical thinking skills at a very young age. They forget that young children are more geared for rote memory—learning facts, learning interesting things about Math, Grammar, History or Science. Public school programs should save the critical thinking for older ages. When children are twelve or thirteen, their brain is more developed to analyze and think critically. Get off the conveyor belt and decide what is best for your children and your family at this time. Don't follow the grade level lists, just to keep up with the government schools.

In conclusion to our rabbit trail, our family has requirements which may be different requirements from your family. To summarize what we require each day: Bible reading as a habit, as well as having a good attitude and developing a solid character foundation. Those requirements lead to the road of righteousness. What requirements do you have in your own family?

WHO MOTIVATES YOU TO LEARN?

If you are really motivated to do something, what is it that inspires you to action?

- Does a speaker who's just a reporter giving you some information inspire you?

- Does a news reporter on TV inspire you?
- Does a friend who can't wait to tell you about an event inspire you?
- Does a pastor who's enthusiastic about his message inspire you?
- Does a workshop leader who overflows with excitement inspire you?

These are great questions to think about. Inspiring my children to desire an education is one of my personal goals. To inspire my children, I think about what kinds of people inspire me? Recently, a local pastor inspired me to not copy the world, but be transformed by the renewing of my mind. When I finish listening to him about a topic, his excitement pours over. I am fired up, ready to apply what God is teaching me. That's the excitement I want to offer to my kids. I want to inspire them, which means I must be involved and excited about the material too.

TIPS TO INSPIRE A LOVE A LEARNING

I f you want to inspire your children to love learning, you might try a variety of ideas. Don't try them all at one time; make simple changes, one at a time. I've included some ideas that I used to inspire my own kids to love learning. Read through them and choose one you can try soon.

GRACE WEEK

In the past, we had Grace Week during the last week of each month. How did that look? The first three weeks of the month, our homeschool was more mom-directed. The last week of the month was child-chosen. Each child chose a subject to study or a project to complete. They spent their days working on their own chosen activity. Additionally, we chose an area of weakness in their school subjects. Every day that week my children works on their area of weakness, as well. It might be learning their multiplication facts, identifying adjectives or something similar. Each child had two areas of study for the week – one academic weakness and one chosen topic. At the end of the week, we had a special dinner. After dinner, each child made a presentation of their chosen study.

This follows the personal growth plan discussed earlier. Set aside time for your child's topic of interest and academic weakness. File quickly what the child learns. Apply what was learned by creating a presentation. Make the presentation at the end of the week. One time, Ashley made a life-size teepee. Another time, Gentry made a gyroscope.

If you are having a hard time breaking away from structured curriculum, Grace Week is a great place to start. Continue doing what you already do, except the last week of each month. Gradually you will be able to hop off the curriculum conveyor belt.

In our family, we are moving forward from Grace Week to allow our children to regularly make more choices about their studies. Here's a method that might work for your family. Let each child choose a topic of interest. When they make a choice about their studies, they are taking one small step to leadership in decision making. Topics may include Jane Austen, basketball, X-box, constellations, motorcycles, cooking. Whatever your child likes is a possible field of study.

Don't discount your children's topics or interests, just because it's not what you think is important. If your child thinks it's important, they will be much more interested in reading and studying. After they choose a topic, your child will write better essays and study more diligently. Let your children choose their topic, so they will be inspired to study better.

Hunter chose to study basketball one week in the spring. We went to the library and let him choose several books. We even found a book about the science of sports. He read all about shooting angles, friction with court shoes and stopping rate when running down the court. He wrote pages about each basketball star. I can't remember the last time he wrote so many paragraphs about a given topic. He was interested in basketball and his work showed it.

– *Choose Topic*

– *Gather Books*

– *Projects*

– *Library*

– *Active*

Can you imagine your child's face if you told him, "Hey, we're going to study Wii this week?" My son would fall off his bed. I am not saying you should play Wii all week long. I'm suggesting you read the history of Wii, learn the reasons for a Wii, research the history of Wii games. You might start with the following questions.

- How do they develop these games?
- How do they come up with these ideas?
- What kind of software do they use?
- What is this whole gaming industry about?

Depending on your child's age, you can study a variety of traditional subjects: Math, History, and Science to study Wii. Now that I've written about it, I might let my son study Wii this year. He would be quite surprised!

Once you choose that topic, study it together if you have younger kids. Independent study is saved for older students. If you are going to inspire your child, you need to be studying with them. If you have ten children, you're probably thinking, "Great, I can't do ten different topics at one time." No, you can't, so make a deal with your children. Tell them you will take turns studying each child's areas of interest...together. As they get older, they can be more independent and study their own areas of interest.

After your children choose a topic, begin to make plans for a variety of activities. If you are interested and excited about their topics, your children will get more excited. You are on the path to inspiring. I know it takes some effort, but it is well worth it.

Go to the library and find all the books you can. Make them age-appropriate for each of your children. If you have younger children, you want to read aloud and discuss as you read. As your children get older, each child will read, write and discuss the given topic. Be sure each child keeps a daily reading journal or copybook from their own readings.

Depending on the topic, you will want to have some hands-on activities. It is quite exciting to have a project to show Dad when he gets home. That's more leadership skills: learning how to give a presentation, learning how to speak in public, learning how to speak up and not stare at the ground when you're speaking. This becomes a lifestyle of learning because the whole family is involved in learning. And above all, make it fun!

FAMILY READING

Besides the books to read silently, choose a book to read as a family. When you read as a family, learning becomes a real part of your family lifestyle. Children see their parents interested in further education even though they are no longer in "school". Education continues as you discuss books and issues. Discussions will emerge at the diner table; it is only natural.

We read the Little Britches series for several years. One week, we were laughing in the van about some of the situations described and how Ralph was dealing with his grandfather. Then we talked about who would want to live with his grandfather. He was a man of no understanding, empathy or sympathy. Since we read this book aloud as a family, we had the chance to talk about relationships with people, with our parents, with our grandparents.

It may seem overwhelming right now, and it might be. If I'm honest, there are plenty of times I can't always pull it together. But, I can always read aloud to my children and discuss those books. If we don't do anything else in a day, we read aloud. I am not going to assign workbooks because of the grade number listed on the cover or because I need busy work to keep my children occupied. If I want to keep my children occupied, I simply choose a book from our book shelf and let them read it silently.

> *Be anxious for nothing, but in everything by prayer and supplication, with thanksgiving, let your requests be made known to God; and the peace of God, which surpasses all understanding, will guard your hearts and minds through Christ Jesus.*
>
> **Philippians 4:6-7**

When you feel overwhelmed, remember why you are using this approach to educate your children. Remember that those educated on the conveyor belt only learn *what to think*. Remember that discussing your read alouds as a family teaches your children *how to think*. Finally, remember that God is standing next to you and will never fail you. Turn to Him for guidance, comfort and wisdom as you raise leaders who know *how to think.*

ROUTINE DAYS

One thing I must keep in mind is not every day is one of excitement. There are days when I go through my routine that God has given me and do it with a thankful, gracious attitude. Seek to inspire your children by showing them how to cheerfully perform daily, routine activities. Your children should be able to complete the day-in and day-out activities with a great attitude. Training cheerful children now will produce pleasant adults in the future.

On the other hand, there is always room to increase your inspiration, excitement, and enthusiasm. How do you do that? I know your children can see when you are truly excited about an activity or topic, whether it's education, hobbies or family activities. Find topics that interest you and your children. As I said earlier, I begin by looking for topics that interest my children, tying their learning in with their interests.

One recent example includes Gentry and Hunter. They both love sports. Last year I took my daughter for her back-to-school lunch before "regular school" starts. We visited a used bookstore and she found a book about Derek Jeter. I told her to put it in our basket. On the first day of school, what was sitting in my son's stack of supplies and materials, but his Derek Jeter biography? He was quite excited about this book.

Gentry also found some books on soccer, so we bought those for her to read as well. They were sitting on her desk the first day of school, too. We talked about her reading those books and researching what makes a good athlete and a good team member. Eventually I want to encourage her to write a paper on those topics. She started this topic almost a year ago but she's never written her paper, which leads me to another point. You might not always finish every study in a year. It's not about "completing the program" in a year. It is okay to continue studying a topic from one year to the next. When I was a school teacher, I don't think I ever finished a textbook in the year.

Back to Gentry. She came up to me towards the end of August and said, "I've found a class I want to take at the college here."

I thought, "Oh, great, I didn't know you wanted to take classes at the local liberal arts college."

She said, "Yes, they have a class on the history of sports." She enrolled in that class and completed her paper from last year. One day she might develop her findings into some sort of research paper.

You should know that the above example is referring to a sixteen-year old, an older student who can study independently. If she was an eight year old who loved sports, I would start with reading many biographies of sports heroes. Look at the character qualities of each athlete and keep a running list. From there an eight year old might write one paragraph about a great athlete.

I hope you see the flexibility you can have with your children's studies. You can be flexible in the given topics, as well as the time period allotted for specific studies. There is no rule written in heaven that says you must complete all studies in a one-year time period. That is only true for the factory school and the conveyor belt students.

Find out what makes you child tick and use it to inspire them to study. Many children are inspired by sports and it's a great avenue to teach character, study skills, and writing skills. If they enjoy what they are reading, they will enjoy talking about it and writing about it, too.

Does this mean your child may not read all the books you have planned? (I'm talking to myself especially.) Yes! It's alright if your children do not read every book you have planned or some curriculum tells you to read. This year I let Hunter choose a book and then I would choose a book. We went back and forth. That way I was able to have him read certain books that I wanted him to read, but I could also inspire him with the books in which he was interested. In fact, Hunter asked me just if we could make more choices about his studies. Of course, we will continue to let him make choices.

For me it is hard to let go, but that's what I need to do sometimes. Do you feel that way at times? When your children are ready to take ownership of their education, it is definitely time to let go. God has a destiny and a calling for each of us and that includes our children. Why not personalize your children's education so they are fulfilling God's calling?

Are you inspired or perspired? Sometimes I am more perspired than inspired. Leadership education takes much time and energy, so I can get very tired. What about you? In the end, I remind myself to look at all the possibilities for my children to mature in Christ.

> *Flex a little bit - Relax!*

I envision some of you saying, "What about the basics? What if they miss a math lesson? What if they don't know what a gerund is in grammar?" Remember, you don't always have to know what a gerund is to use a gerund. You need to flex a little bit and relax.

MATH CLASSICS THAT INSPIRE

Classics can inspire, even in math. Am I crazy? Classics in math? No, I'm not crazy. This year we read math books with great stories that teach mathematical concepts. When I was planning, I flipped through some books from our discontinued rack. I found a book called *Math Trek* and thought this might work for my twelve year old, especially since he lost math workbook

Math Trek has about seven or eight chapters. Each chapter focuses on a mathematical concept or math puzzles. The first chapter is all about knots. Hunter uses a string to see if the loops drawn on the page would really knot or unknot. After going through several of these, he discovers there are fake knots, as well as cool information about knots. He works through three more chapters before I realized how far he had gone in *Math Trek*. He loves this book. In fact he came up a week later and says, "Mom, is there a *Math Trek Two*?"

I had to tell him, "I didn't know. The reason we're using this one is that it didn't sell at the book sales last year. Aren't you glad it didn't sell?" He never complained about doing his math studies that week. We still need to find his math workbook, which we did eventually find. My thought is to alternate between math workbooks and living math stories.

If you're trying to figure out a book that would help you inspire Math, I highly recommend *Mathematicians Are Real People, Too*. We started reading one chapter a week in January. Each chapter has a short biography of a famous mathematician.

The first chapter we read was Thales. Thales figured out how to measure the height of a pyramid by using shadows and ratios. The ratio of Thales' shadow to his height, compared to the shadow of the pyramid determined the height of the pyramid. When we finished the chapter, we sat on the bed with paper, figuring out all sorts of ratios. Did they have to complete math workbooks to learn how to use ratios? No. Ratios became real life after we tried some on paper.

The next chapter was about Pythagoras. My girls knew the Pythagorean Theorem, but Hunter did not. He did know what the square of a number was, so he understood the concept of squares. He was introduced to the concept of the Pythagorean Theorem as we read about Pythagoras. Next he read *What's Your Angle, Pythagoras?*, which gave him an understanding of the Pythagorean Theorem. Where did Hunter learn the Pythagorean Theorem? Not from a math workbook, but from a math story book.

OTHER INSPIRING BOOKS

If you want to inspire your children in science, find topics of interest. Gather science books and start doing activities. Science at the young age should always be hands-on discovery. Usually your public library has many science books at the elementary ages that includes simple activities.

Inspire your children by

– *using classics*

– *using real life*

– *giving your children a reason why*

From there, introduce stories of the scientists. We did a whole unit on astronomy by using a Christian based astronomy book, lots of library books, an experiment book, and a biography about Galileo. I even designed some grammar pages based on astronomy concepts. Hunter loved it because he could choose his silent reading books. .

In history there are too many classics to even list here. My favorite resource is the *The Best Books Of All Time*, written by Gentry. In our booth at homeschool conventions, many moms ask Gentry her opinion of historical books. So she compiled a list of her favorite books she read the last ten years. Gentry was sixteen years old when she compiled her list, so it's from a homeschooler's perspective.

My favorite aspect of *Truth Quest History* is its list of books in chronological order, interspersed with Biblical worldview comments When you use *Truth Quest*, you are constantly looking at who is God to that civilization and who is mankind, based on their beliefs. Failures are just as important to study as successes in history. Your children will learn more from their own failures, than their successes. Likewise, they will learn from historical failures.

Inspire your children by using classics, using real life, and giving your children a reason why. If I don't know a reason why my children are studying a particular subject, then I will not waste my time teaching it to them. You ought to have a clear vision why you're teaching specific subjects and topics.

PRACTICAL DAILY TIPS

Are you looking for specific, practical ways to inspire your children to love learning? Look no further because I've included nine practical tips you can use today with your own family. I do not recommend doing all nine immediately. Simply choose one of these tips you can use to inspire your own children. Gradually add others as you see them fit your family.

A reminder to parents of high school aged students that don't love learning: start here. Do not jump into independent study with older children unless they love learning. Spend some time, even a whole semester or year, developing a love for learning in your children. Do not succumb to the pressure to finish every high school subject and textbook available. Develop integrity, perseverance, humility and a love of learning before you move into independent studies.

GROUP READING TIME

Start your day by reading as a family. I call this Group Reading Time. It is a time where you meet together (mom with children), read classics together, discuss history together, read living math books together, or study fine arts or music. This is a time for you to teach your children things that you are learning and are excited about. Spend this time sharing what is important to you. Be sure to find books that interest your children so they will enjoy this time.

Even though I listed some topics for this group time, our topics vary from month-to-month and year-to-year. We always read aloud a classic book and discuss history because that is important to me. If I wait until later in the day for these activities, they are not always completed.

Several years ago I decided to start our day with my highest priority – reading aloud. When I first started our group time, complaining ensued. My children were concerned they wouldn't finish their math assignment. I reassured them group reading time was most important to me. We will work through the changes in our schedule. I stood my ground and Group Reading Time is a habit in all of our lives. We even read aloud in the mornings on days we aren't having formal academics. This is a great way to continue studies throughout the summer, if you usually take a break. Believe it or not, our teens still join us for Group Reading Time.

Use Group Reading Time for whatever is most important to you. God calls families to different areas, so follow His direction as you decide what to do. Your Group Time will look different than mine. Hop off the conveyor belt and educate your children with your priorities.

CAR SCHOOL – KITCHEN SCHOOL

During the first year of homeschooling my daughters, we sent my son to kindergarten at a private school. I continued volunteering at the school. One day while I was volunteering, Ashley & Gentry brought their home-school activities. One of the moms said, "Oh, do you car school?" I had never heard that term before, but it's really true. We do school everywhere. Hopefully, you're learning all day long so it's not really school, but just a love of learning.

When you are cleaning up after a meal, talk to your children about what they're learning. When you are making dinner or lunch, have a discussion, give oral exams or coach your children along as they work nearby.

If you're in the car, listen to CDs to enrich your children and introduce them to music, lectures, stories and more. Some of our favorite CDs include the following. You can read or see my review in the resources section.

- Classical Kids Music
- Henty Books on Tape
- Greathall Productions

To be more interactive as you drive along, discuss your children's studies. If you're all learning about the same topic, then you're all on the same page in the car. No matter where you are driving, to soccer practice or a weekend getaway, you can discuss your studies from the previous week. I've even done grammar in the car, talking about nouns and adjectives.

FAMILY DEVOTIONS

A simple way to start your day together is eating breakfast, followed by devotions. If Dad can join you for breakfast, you should feel blessed. If not, find a time when you can have your daily devotions as a family. You need to set

Family Devotions
- *Our 24 Family Ways*
- *Training Hearts, Teaching Minds*
- *Making Biblical Decisions*

aside a time in your day for devotions and commit to put everything else aside. For our family, we have family devotions after we eat breakfast. We are blessed to have Dad home at that time so he can lead those devotions.

Why do we have family devotions at breakfast? It ties devotions to something we won't miss – a meal. Steve eats quickly and starts reading while the rest of us finish our meal.

If Dad is not interested in leading family devotions, do not nag him about it. Find a time during the day when you can lead devotions with your children. Do not make a big deal about this. Begin praying for your husband to take an interest in leading devotions. Then, wait to see God's work in your lives. Be sure to note that waiting can take years. Please don't expect an instant change in this area of your life. Be faithful leading your children in devotions and wait patiently.

I know from experience. Steve and I were on different pages about family devotions when the kids were little. He wanted it to be organic; I wanted it to be planned. I nagged for awhile, but God quickly convicted to stop nagging. I started praying instead. After Steve left for work, I led devotions with the kids. I did not make a big deal of devotions in front of Steve. I led quietly.

I prayed and I prayed and I prayed. No change in a week. No change in a month. No change in a year. It was several years before we were on the same page. Steve decided that organic devotions was not happening, so he needed to be more intentional. He tied our family devotions to breakfast because we ate breakfast together each morning. Breakfast was already a habit, so adding devotions to a habit helped make reading the Bible daily a habit also.

DINNER TIME

Eat dinner together! Let me say that again, eat dinner together!

Dinner time is a must for families who want to interact with each other and bond together. I know you have a hectic schedule and there is always someone missing around dinner time. Baseball practice, dance lessons, piano and the like eat away our schedule so we are not together in the evenings. If these are a hindrance to family time at dinner, evaluate what is most important. Is it family time or individual activities? You may need to drop one of those many activities in which your children participate.

To find a way to all eat dinner together, you may need to step back. I know it is difficult because our family had seasons where all three children were in three different activities. One winter, we did not eat until 8:30 or 9:00 at night! We had a little snack at 5:30 and eventually sat down at the dinner table together around 8:30. More important than eating at a normal dinner time was eating together. Make a choice: eat together or eat at six with family members missing.

For those of you with large families, you must think about the babies that usually go to bed at eight. Be creative with your schedule and re-evaluate the other children's activities.

The dinner table needs to be a daily part of your lifestyle. It's a great way to find out about one another's days, discuss current events, argue about who the best basketball player is or discover what God's Word says about a problem you are encountering. It's Open Forum time at our dinner table.

EVENINGS TOGETHER

Spend your evenings together as a family by reading books aloud, watching a baseball game, playing a game together, watching a good movie, or going for a walk. Make this routine from the time your children are little, so they want to be home in the evenings when they are older.

We had several outside opportunities for Ashley one year of high school. During the fall, she wanted to attend every party or study session available. As the year rolled by, she realized it was more important to stay home. What an encouragement to me when she made this decision on her own! I am not saying your children should stay home and never visit friends or go to parties. Help your older ones look at their schedule and find ways to be home regularly. When my daughter found out which nights we would be home, she planned her study group on a different night. She began to value our time together and even sacrifice to be home.

NOTEBOOKING

At this age, your children should keep notebooks and lapbooks. This is a meaningful way for everyone to see what has been learned over the past year. It's also a great tool for grandmas. Grandmas aren't always sure what you're doing when you jump off the conveyor belt in you homeschool. If you have a notebook showing all your children learns over the year, grandparents are calmed in their concerns.

Notebooks include writing assignment, timelines, calendars, experiments, activities, pictures of activities, awards and other momentos from

4 R's of Notebooking

– *Research*

– *Reason*

– *Relate*

– *Record*

the year. One method is having a notebook for each year. Yearly notebooks offer a sense of accomplishment, as well as a reminder that it's time to move on. Another method to notebooking is having a notebook for each subject studied. From year-to-year, your child includes studies in that subject area.

If you want to use notebooking to integrate a Biblical perspective, I recommend the four R's of notebooking.

1. **Research**

Start with researching God's word. Go to Scripture and see what God has to say about your studied topic or the book you are reading. Let's look at a few examples. If you are reading a book about evolution, go to the creation stories in Genesis 1 & 2. Look at what God says about that topic. Research evolution & creation from the Bible first. Or, maybe you are studying Ancient Egypt. Read the story of the Exodus and relate it to Ancient Egypt history

2. **Reasoning**

Draw and apply principles as you reason through the studied subject and the Bible research. This encourages your kids to really think. Kids move from researching a subject area to reasoning and drawing a conclusions. This is a higher level thinking process. Younger children may simply draw their conclusions. Older kids can write out their reasoning – cause and effect, conclusions, opinions and so forth.

3. **Relate**

Relate these truths and principles that are discovered in the subject area, as well as the student's character.

We may be the best Christian parents ever to teach our children Bible lessons. Build that relationship and cultivate excellent readers and writers for the Lord. We must

also teach them the history of God's hands in developing
a nation where the church and the individual has experi-
enced the greatest liberty to achieve God's best. Other-
wise, we have failed.

— Lori Harris

We can teach all the Bible concepts in the world. But if we're not relating it to real life, to your children, to life that's going on around them, we are not doing our job as homeschool parents. This may be a difficult task at first. Model how you would relate the research & reasoned truths. As you model this process, your children can imitate you and begin to relate truths & principles on their own.

4. **Record**

It's okay if each child has a different record of what they're learning. That's the beauty of research-reason-relate. If you are notebooking about Swiss Family Robinson, you may have one child who relates the story to work ethic in the family. Another child might be impressed with the wildlife and the way God created nature. Let them have different records of their findings. It's OK… I promise!

In the end, teachers and students should record individual application of the Biblical principles to each subject area. Recording makes a big impact on your kids. It imprints deeply on their minds and their memory, so they remember the concepts they learned. Record in your notebook as a final part of notebooking.

In summary, we're simply identifying the Biblical worldview of each subject. We need to remember that each subject area was created by God and will reveal His story of cause and effect in the events of man and nations throughout time.

6 TYPES OF NOTEBOOKS IN YOUR HOMESCHOOL

Before we move to lapbooking, I want to share 6 types of notebooks you might use in your leadership homeschool.

Bible Notebooks

What about a Bible Notebook? How would you start a Bible Notebook? Start at the beginning. If your kids are little, find a good storybook of Bible stories. Let your kids illustrate each story and write a caption underneath their picture. As they get older, you read directly from the bible. Use your regular Bible reading. We start in the Old Testament and move forward.

When your kids are young, illustrate and write a brief narration of that particular story. As your kids get older, start a Bible journal. They can write a summary of what was read during family devotions. Or, they can keep a notebook about what they are learning personally in the bible.

---

6 Types of Notebooks

1. Bible Notebook

2. Literature Notebook

3. Copywork & Dictation Notebook

4. Writing Notebook

5. History Notebook

6. Science Notebook

Proverbs is a great book for both the young men and young women, in their teen years. Read two or three verses in Proverbs. Then each teen writes down what they learned from those verses and how it applies to their lives.

Another option is a Concordance study. Give your kids a word to look up in a concordance. Write down what they discover from each verse where that word is used. Then, draw conclusions. If you're not sure where to get started, I would say maybe the word "save" or "righteousness" or "wise".

One of my favorite Concordance studies is salvation or saved. As you work through verses with salvation or saved in them, you ought to ask yourself, "Saved from what. We usually think of saved as simply saved from the penalty of sin. I'm going to heaven and I'm saved. But saved is used a lot of other ways. Someone in a boat is saved from drowning. Or someone else is saved from starvation. Look at the context as you do any Concordance study.

Literature Notebooks

What about a Literature notebook? Again, I would start very small. At first, simply record the titles of each book your child reads on their own. When they are ready, they can illustrate a book or give a short synopsis. Or, illustrate one aspect of a book, such as a character or the setting. You might also include a book report or book review. Another option is to include 2 or 3 of your child's narrations, with a final summary narration.

As your students get older, they should interact with the book. This is very similar to journaling. Record some of the questions & answers you've discussed about a book. Or, write about how well the author practiced his craft. How well the characters were developed. Did the author paint scenes very well?

Copywork & Dictation Notebooks

Copybooks & Dictation notebooks are some of the easiest notebooks to start. You might remember Benjamin Franklin worked on a copybook when he was in his teens. Most homeschoolers think copywork is for 5, 6, and 7 year olds, but this is not true.

Historically, Franklin used the idea of imitation in writing as a young adult. This helped him improve his writing ability. It is very similar to the strategy taught by Teaching Writing: Structure & Style. Franklin read books, then rewrote it in his own words. Copywork notebooks might follow this progression:

- Tracing letters
- Copy words
- Copy sentences
- Copy paragraphs
- Read paragraphs – Rewrite in your own words
- Dictation of sentences & paragraphs

On top of copying the passage, your kids can illustrate the copy assignment. You might also illustrate the dictation passage, as well. As you look for copywork & dictation exercises, be sure you use a wide variety of sources: Scripture passages, well-written lines, poetry, favorite literature passages, quotes, historical speeches. You could even study Science theories if you like.

Writing Notebook

A Writing notebook can last a long time and be used as a history of your child's writing. Your kids ought to be writing everyday. We kept a notebook for all my children's finished drafts. Two of my favorite writing programs are WriteShop and Institute for Excellence in Writing. You can read my review of each program here: http://HowToHomeschoolMyChild.com/writing-reviews

Most types of writings you include in a writing notebook are included in both of the resources listed above. You'll find descriptive writing, biographies, book reviews, news stories, research paper, character sketches, poems, short stories that are included in a writing notebook.

History Notebook

With a History notebook, you might organize entries in chronological order. I suggest including maps, timelines & narrations. Rely on biographies and good historical fiction to tell the story with narrations. Rarely, if ever, read textbooks. As we read historical books, my kids would narrate to me. When young, I wrote down their narration for them to copy into their notebooks. Older children can write their own narration for the stories that we were reading.

Remember to include entries about Bible History or Church History right alongside secular history. So if you're studying ancient Egypt, include entries about Moses and the exodus from Egypt.

As your kids get older and their thinking skills get better, start writing comparisons and contrasts about circumstances in history. This may include different leaders or different places, cause and effect, especially when it comes to battles and wars. With notebooks, you inspire much critical thinking. If you are going on field trips, include pictures of places you visit. Then, you have a history of your studies, like a scrapbook of history.

Science Notebook

In Science, have kids draw diagrams or illustrations about scientific topics. When your kids are old enough to complete experiments, start recording their findings in your experiments. These recordings can be in either picture or written format. Use either format to show what happened with your science experiments. We used our notebook at the high school level for our lab reports. We used a specific lab report form for each experiment

Another aspect of Science notebooks includes information about famous scientists. Read biographies of scientists that are related to the scientific topics. If you are studying astronomy, read about Galileo. If you are studying gravity, read a biography of Sir Isaac Newton. For each scientist, include a paragraph or short story about that particular scientists.

The best resource I found to help you make notebooks is Notebooking Pages. You can test drive it with their free sampler right here: http://How-ToHomeschoolMyChild.com/notebooking

LAPBOOKS

Lapbooking is an easy way to present the information your children learn in unschooling. You might be saying to yourself, "I'm not quite sure what a lapbook is."

Cathy Duffy offers an excellent explanation of lapbooks.

> *Lap Books offer creative ways for children to record information they are learning and create attractive presentations of that information, as well as use the information to study. A Lap Book is essentially a creatively folded manila file folder with lots of smaller creatively cut and folded pieces of paper that are attached in different ways. This loose definition reflects the realm of creative options that might be used to create lap books.*
>
> *http://cathyduffyreviews.com/parent-helps/ultimate-lap-book-handbook.htm*

An example of a lapbook might be one about Reptiles. You have a pocket or a booklet about the Chameleons, one about Venomous Snakes, one about What to do when Bitten by a Snake, another about Turtles. Whatever you're interested in learning about reptiles is included in your lapbooks.

Making Lapbooks

You can use poster board or card stock as your lapbook, but we often would use manila folders as the base of our lapbook. Manila folders make a very nice, sturdy lapbook where you can cut out pockets and pieces to glue on the lapbook. If your children make many lapbooks, you might color code them by using colored manila folders. For instance, blue is Reading and Literature, red is History, green is Science and so forth. I've also seen several lapbooks done in a single sketch book because the paper is heavier than regular paper. As you open up each page, you have a mini-lapbook. You might do this as a modified notebook. When you are studying art history, let each open page represent an artist. Add pockets & pieces to insert information about that artist.

You might choose to have one lapbook for each child or you may choose to do one lapbook for the whole family. Do what works best for your family. Your lapbook will record what is learned. Some of the ideas to include in your lapbooks are vocabulary words, concepts being learned, timelines, diagrams, maps, & lists.

Realize that all your vocabulary words aren't done in one day. You can have a pocket for vocabulary. Insert slips of paper with a new vocabulary word each day. Encourage your child to use that word in conversation each day, as well as his writing each day.

In our Ancient Greece example, each child puts a new word in the pocket everyday for a week. At the end of the week, your child should use all of his new words in a paragraph about Ancient Greece. The best way to learn vocabulary is to use new vocabulary words in conversation and in writing. With a history lapbook such as Ancient Greece, might have a timeline where you fill out the timeline across the top of your lapbooks. Include the years of major events in Ancient Greece. Other pockets in your lapbook may include information about the culture, the food, the slavery, the architecture, the arts.

Lapbooking Supplies

You don't want to be running around for a half an hour, trying to gather all the supplies you need for lapbooks. Get a big Rubbermaids to keep your lapbooking supplies. Keep it next to you art supply box and your science experiment supply box.

What will you need to make lapbooks?

Obviously you're going to need scissors and glue – lots of scissors, glue or glue sticks. You'll also need colored paper, construction paper or card stock. For the base of your lapbook, I suggest manila folders or large art books. From there, make a box with your other supplies: colored pencils, felt tip markers, and small ready-made booklets of different shapes and sizes.

Envelopes are a great to put in this bucket of supplies. Glue down the side we normally address. On the flap side, you can open it up and insert slips of paper or index cards with the information your child learned.

Keep a Ziploc filled with ribbons, stickers, rubber stamps, glitter, art supplies, & other fun ways to decorate your lapbooks. A box of giant Ziplocs can be used to keep the entire lapbook as your child works on it. They won't necessarily have everything glued down everyday. So they place their in-progress lapbook with all the pieces in the Ziploc. Label the Ziploc with each child's name. The next day, each child pulls out their lapbook and starts working. Everyday, it all goes back in that child's Ziploc.

One of my favorite resources for lapbooking is *A Journey through Learning*. You can even get a free lapbook to try it out & see if it's a good fit for your family. Use this link to get your free lapbook.

http://HowToHomeschoolMyChild.com/lapbooking

LEARNING GAMES

Is it hard to keep your kids' attention in your homeschool? Do you struggle to make learning fun? If you answered yes to either of these questions,

I completely understand. I've always believed that kids retain more when they are interacting with the subject being studied. Plus, competition in games usually motivates kids to remember the material. This was especially true for my son. Hunter wanted to keep playing a game until he was the winner. If you have sons, I'm sure you can relate!

My kids want to have fun learning, so I was always searching for the best learning games for kids. Children learn faster and retain more when they are having fun! Animal classification becomes a snap when you are trying to make a match before your sister does. These days you can find games that cover almost every subject area you might study. Playing these games as a family after dinner is a great way to spend time together and reduce the amount of time spent in front of the one-eyed monster (your television)!

As you play games together, your children learn without realizing it. Just the other day, Hunter and I played a game about animal habitats. Before you knew it, we both learned about polar regions, tropical forests, and other areas. Games are a great way to inspire your children to learn.

Some years we had enough money to buy specific games for topics we were studying. Other years, we didn't have that much money. So, I used simple, creative, learning games for kids that I could make at home. Let me share a few of our homemade learning games.

Balloon Memory Game

Kids love this game because there is so much fun activity. Moms & teachers love this game because it's a great review game for any topic you are studying. How does it work?

1. On slips of paper, write down questions & answers for topic studied. Or any other review items, such as vocabulary words/definitions or ordering a list.
2. Insert the slips of paper in balloons.
3. Blow up the balloons & tie.
4. Let your kids pop the balloons.
5. Kids match questions and answers or vocabulary words with definitions or putting in order a list or putting items under specific groups.

In El Salvador I used this game to review memory verses. The verse is broken into phrases. Each phrase is inserted into a balloon. Once the team pops all the balloons, they must put the verse phrases in correct order. You can use whatever information you want to review in your balloons.

Domino Review Game

On the back of dominoes, write words or phrases. These words will be used to match, list or order. It's similar to the balloon game. We've also used dominoes to review memory verses by writing words/phrases on the back of dominoes. Once you have the words on the back of each domino, place the dominoes on the table with the dots upward. Shuffle around the dominoes to mix them up.

Countdown to let the kids start (3-2-1). Kids turn over the dominoes and match / list / order the words & phrases.

- Other ideas for using dominoes to review:
- Match states & capitals
- Math facts with solutions
- Geometric shapes with names
- Vocabulary words with definition (in any subject area)
- Putting animals in correct animal group
- Sorting parts of speech (words on dominoes must go under headings of noun, verb, adjective, adverb or any other grammar concept)
- You get the idea . . .

Lego or Duplos Review Game

Using a dry erase marker write math facts on the sides of legos or duplos. (Duplos are easier for this game because they are larger) Write the solution on other legos. Jumble up the legos. Let your kids match the math fact with the solution by placing the solution lego on top of the math fact. You can also stack items in a group such as parts of speech or animal groups and so forth.

Jeopardy

When I taught school, my kids loved this game. It does take a little more prep work but it's worth the effort. You may use this for any & all subject areas. To make this simple, you can use a whiteboard and write your headings directly on the whiteboard. Along the top of the board write the topics you will review. If you are reviewing all subjects, you can write math, grammar, history, science. Along the left side of the board, write the points value such as 100, 200, 300, 400, 500.

You can use envelopes for pockets. On each envelope pocket, write the number of points awarded for answering that question correctly. For our example, you'll need 4 envelopes with 100 written on it, 4 envelopes with 200 and so on. Tape each envelope in the correct row. Now it's time to write review questions on index cards. On the back of each card, write the answer. Place each question in a pocket. Place the easier questions in the smaller points value; harder questions receive larger number of points.

Divide into 2 teams, taking turns to choose a question to answer. When it is the student's turn, they choose a topic and points value. Mom (or teacher) reads the question in that pocket. If answered correctly, that team receives the number of points on the envelope/pocket. If not, mom gives the correct answer. Play moves back and forth, from team to team. The team with the most points wins.

Fun Games
- *Balloon Memory Game*
- *Domino Review Game*
- *Legos or Duplos Review Game*
- *Jeopardy*
- *Plastic Easter Egg Learning Games*

Plastic Easter Egg Learning Games

During the springtime, you might try playing games with those cheap Easter eggs. Here are a few ideas to use make learning games from plastic Easter eggs.

- Number eggs. Find odds and place them in number order. Use an egg carton to hold your eggs.
- Match clock with time
- Label eggs with letters so you have enough letters for your spelling words. Call out your spelling list and let your child use the eggs to spell the words. Place the word in your egg carton. If you don't want to call the words yourself, use a program like Phonetic Zoo Spelling. Pop in the cd and they will call out your spelling list.
- Match states & capitals
- Match fraction with decimals.
- Match rhyming words
- Match capital letter with lower case letter
- Make compound words
- Work on fine motor skills by using your plastic Easter egg as a scoop. Scoop up dried beans or sand or peanuts. If you scoop up an item like beans or peanuts, have your child count how many they scoop each time.
- Number your eggs by 5's or 10's or odds/evens. Hide the eggs. Once your childrne find all the eggs, make a train of Easter eggs with the numbers in correct order.
- Sort your eggs by odd numbers & even numbers.
- Match stickers with words
- Match number with dots
- Fill eggs with different items. Let your child shake the egg and guess what is inside.
- Sort your eggs by color.

As a former public school teacher and homeschool mom, I highly recommend using learning games to help your students retain information. I know my kids learned more from learning games than me talking to them.

BOOKSHELVES

Bookshelves are a must when you hop off the conveyor belt. If your children have a difficult time reaching their books, they will become discouraged to read. When they are young, books ought to be part of your toy box. As they get older, you ought to have books on a wide variety of topics for your children to enjoy. Use the lower shelves for easy readers, simple science experiment books, short biographies, and so on. As your children get older, you will want to have those upper shelves a little more organized by categories of study.

Take a look at your bookshelves and evaluate if they are enticing to your children. Look at your bookshelves from your children's point of view, not your own. If you were a child, would you want to spend time next to your bookshelf, pulling down books to read?

PERSONALIZE

The last tip in this section is personalization. It is not the last tip to inspire a love of learning, just the last one on this list. You need to get off the conveyor belt and out of the factory school model so you can personalize your child's education. Isn't it worth it to make sure your child's education geared towards his calling?

Remember it is okay to alter what you're doing, if it fits into your goals. You need to evaluate your goals for each child at least annually. About twice a year my husband and I go out on a dinner date to talk about our children and their needs at the time. Just so you moms know – I am the one who initiates this discussion each time. My husband is totally interested in our children and their maturity, but he does not initiate this type of discussion. I remind you of this scenario so you don't get upset with your spouse when he isn't initiating conversation about your children's studies.

I have a friend who meets with her husband each morning about 6:00 am to talk about their children. Meeting on a daily basis helps you stay on top of things with their children. It also encourages your conversation about positives with your children, not just problems. If this works, great. If not, don't nag your husband about meeting so early in the morning. Trust God for direction in your homeschool and your spouse's ideas.

As the primary homeschool teacher, stay up with your children's needs. If something is not working, change it so it does work. You are not married to every method and activity that you choose to do. You ARE the expert about your child, not the scope-and-sequence, not the factory school, and especially not the conveyor belt.

If you don't remember anything else, remember to get off the conveyor belt and personalize your children's education according to their needs and God's calling for each of them.

SHIFTING TO INDEPENDENCE

ARE YOUR CHILDREN READY?

As your children get older, they will become more independent in their studies and learning. Hopefully you have given them the tools of learning as a youngster. Now, they are ready for more in-depth reading, writing, and discussing.

> *Independent studies are the very essence of leadership education*

Independent studies are the very essence of leadership education. But beware! Do not push your children into independent study before they're ready. Many moms start school at an early age. They want to push, push, push academics, while actually turning off your children to love learning. You can do the same if you push your children to independent studies too early.

When your children complete their years of independent study in homeschooling, they should have the tools to learn the rest of their lives. By this time, your children should have a desire for learning, the ability to make wise decisions, the ability to process information and present information. All of these leadership qualities are necessary for your children to make wise decisions, process information and present information.

ARE YOUR CHILDREN READY?

To determine if your child is ready for independent studies, watch for signs of independence and the ability to work independently. A few questions you should ask yourself are these.

- Can he do his household jobs without being reminded constantly?
- Can he follow directions and complete a task?
- Can he read independently for an extended period of time?

Even though your children may work independently at home, you may wonder if they will continue being responsible with other studies. One year, Ashley took a class which required much independent reading and writing. I was excited to see how well she did, even without our help. After being in this class for awhile, I realized she had really gained the tools of learning. Like all of us, she still learns new tools for study, but it was rewarding to see how well she was able to study on her own.

Even during this time of shifting to independence, there are times when you will require certain studies in your family. Based on family priorities, you will have areas of study that your children must complete. For our family, Bible training, character development and reading is required throughout all their years in our homeschool. As our children mature in their thinking, we have other subjects we want them to study. Actually, we only require one or two subject areas each year. We do not want to require a large variety so that our children do not have enough time to study their own interests.

In the older years as they study independently, they also study Humanities. Humanities includes a Biblical worldview of history, literature, science, theology, philosophy, art, and music. At this age, they practice writing on a regular basis. Many opportunities are given in Humanities and Great Books for writing. These are family requirements; the other studies are chosen by our children.

I remember one year when Gentry chose to study Algebra, Biology and Astronomy while Ashley chose to study Theology, Greek and Astronomy.

You may be wondering about those other subjects. Are you surprised that we allowed our child to make her own choice about Algebra and Biology? Gentry wants to attend college and knows these are requirements to enter college. She's thinking ahead.

WHEN TO SHIFT

Around the ages of twelve to fourteen, students shift to more independent studies. This is an important time to personalize your children's studies. Find the strengths and interests of those children and go from there. During transition to independence, mom is still involved in academics as she becomes a guide.

Projects and presentations are key during this progression to independence. Projects involve a variety of learning activities. When your children have a project, they will perform research, hands-on activities, and presentation of their research. Projects are partly independent and partly guided. As you guide your child through his project, watch to be sure he is comfortable with the amount of independent work required.

If you have a child in transition time that becomes overwhelmed, then take a step back. You don't have to push them yet. As the parent, you know when your child is overwhelmed or when your child is being lazy. If they're overwhelmed, take a step back.

Beyond projects and presentations, treat your children as young adults during this transition time. Give them real responsibilities. Beware not to load their whole day with chores and jobs. Too much responsibility reduces the time to study. Find a balance between real responsibilities and real research.

Continue reading out loud to children at this age. In my opinion, no one is too old to listen as you read books aloud. Stories are loved by all, so take advantage of books while your children are still at home, even when they are teens.

Extra-curricular activities can have a positive or negative effect. If your child is in too many outside activities, you no are no longer the one

influencing your child. Be careful not to enroll in several outside activities as they reduce your influence as well as your priorities. Yet, outside
classes promote accountability which leads to independence. They also
allow opportunities for your child to grow in decision making when you
are not with them.

Sports play a key role in many young men's upbringing. One year,
Hunter played football and basketball. He also took Latin at the boys
school. It was a small class where the teacher only spoke Latin in the
classroom. Although it was a wonderful opportunity to learn, the greatest
benefit was the class pushed my son further than I was pushing him during
this transition time. It made him accountable to someone else and responsible for his own subjects and study. Thus, a positive impact was made on
my son. Look at individual classes and activities to be sure they influence
your child positively.

PROJECTS & PRESENTATIONS

Awhile back, I received a review copy of *Unit Studies Made Easy* . By the
time I finished reviewing it, I was inspired to do our own unit. My first
thought was to find a topic in which my thirteen year old son had an interest. I was fired up and I wanted him to be fired up, also. He and I recently
talked about studying astronomy, but we had never done anything about
it. Once we started discussing our unit, he was excited to study astronomy.

What he was most excited about was choosing which books he would
read. Usually I try to alternate his choice with my choice. The upcoming
week he would get to choose all the books to read. He read about stars,
constellations, nebulae, and all sorts of other astronomical topics. If you
recall, this thirteen year old is not one who chooses to sit down and read.
He would much rather be outside shooting baskets or bothering his sisters.
When we went to the library, I left him on his own while I went to find a
book for myself. I looked down the aisle and saw him bringing about six to
ten books to check out from the library. Normally, he checks out one book
and doesn't always finish that one.

I am reminded that libraries are important when homeschooling. Take advantage of them and make your library visits a weekly routine. Your children will grow up around books and develop a love of reading.

Once we returned home from the library, we gathered all of his books with our personal books about astronomy. Through the week we performed some experiments and projects. I even made up a grammar activity. I took a paragraph from one of his books, typed it up, made some grammar errors in the paragraphs and gave him a copy of it. He had to correct the errors by editing the paragraph and making it correct. All in all, the astronomy unit was successful.

DAYDREAMING

Occasionally, you might see your children at this age daydreaming when they should be studying. John Gatto has an interesting take on daydreaming. John Gatto was the New York State Teacher of the Year twice. After receiving this award, he enlightened the public about what really happens in public schools, writing a tome on the underground history of American education.

Gatto is an excellent teacher with the following comment.

> *When I see kids daydreaming in school, I am careful never to shock them out of their reverie. What I have to say can wait.*

Is this a change from you our education paradigm? When your children start to daydream, let them do it for awhile. Give them a little space. You never know what great ideas they may come up with. When they finish daydreaming, why not talk to them about what they were thinking? Too often you squelch their curiosity at this transition time with too much research and bookwork.

Your children have a lifetime for research and study. Make this transition to independent study a hands-on time for research. Continue studying those areas that are part of your family's priorities, along with topics in which your child is interested.

If you want to move on with independent studies in leadership education, read my book, *Teach Your Children How to Think with Mentoring.* Learn how to mentor your children with classics and real life. Discover how to teach your children to think for themselves while studying on their own.

IN REVIEW

Leadership education begins with you. As parent and teacher, you model for your kids an attitude towards homeschooling and life in general. Take time to work through the steps outlined in this book as you implement leadership education.

1. Write down your strategic vision, strategic mission, strategic motivation
2. Begin your own personal growth plan
3. Develop strong character in your children as you raise them to Godliness
4. Create a love of learning environment in your homeschool
5. Transition your children from dependence on you to more independent studies.

I will close with the 10 reasons I chose leadership education for our homeschool.

1. Teaches our kids to think Biblically & critically
2. Character is paramount & taught at early ages. If older kids do not exhibit Godly character, parents are encouraged to work on character before pursuing academics.

3. Gives my kids the tools of learning so they can learn anything, anywhere.
4. Gives my kids a love of learning
5. High priority of reading & discussing classic books
6. Provides resource rich environment for learning
7. Mentors older kids with classic books & reading journals
8. Socratic dialogue about studies encourages critical thinking
9. Older kids choose studies, thus developing leadership skills
10. Writing activities at all ages, with tools to improve writing

LEADERSHIP EDUCATION RESOURCES

To read and see reviews of these resources, go to
http://HowToHomeschoolMyChild.com/leadership-resources

FREE STUDY GUIDE FOR RAISING LEADERS, NOT FOLLOWERS

As mentioned on the cover, you can receive a free study guide for this book with thought provoking questions and guides for discussions with other homeschoolers. Get your FREE guide here:
http://HowToHomeschoolMyChild.com/leader-study-guide

BIBLIOGRAPHY

Bluedorn, Harvey & Laurie, *Teaching the Trivium*

DeMille, Oliver, *A Thomas Jefferson Education*

Gatto, John, *A Different Kind of Teacher*

Gatto, John, *Underground History of American Education*

Kern, Andrew, *Cultivating Wisdom through Writing*

Maxwell, John, *Developing the Leaders Around You*

Maxwell, John, *The 21 Irrefutable Laws of Leadership*

Myers, Jeff, *Coaching and Mentoring Students*

Schwartz, David, *The Magic of Thinking Big*

CHRISTIAN LEADERSHIP PACKAGE

Get Kerry's entire Christian Leadership package which includes the following:

- *Raising Leaders, Not Followers* ebook
- *Teach Your Children "How to Think" with Mentoring* ebook
- *Hop Off the Conveyor Belt: Tips & Stories* ebook
- *Raising Leaders, Not Followers* Workshop video & transcript
- *Teach Your Children "How to Think" with Mentoring* Workshop video & transcript
- *Classic Book Lists* (Children, Youth, Adult)
- *Help for the Harried Homeschooler*: Schedule & Lists for Raising Leaders

Total Value $132   Paperback Owner Special $27

http://HowToHomeschoolMyChild.com/rlnf-paperback-special

RESOURCES FOR EACH APPROACH TO CHRISTIAN HOMESCHOOLING

If you want specific resources that Kerry recommends for each approach to Christian homeschooling, you may be interested in one of the following resources.

Get it everything you need to decide which approach is best for your family when you invest in . . .

Approaches to Christian Homeschooling Complete Package

- Approaches to Christian Homeschooling ebook
- Approaches to Christian Homeschooling Resource Guide (with clickable links)
- 8 Video Workshops on each approach (digital)

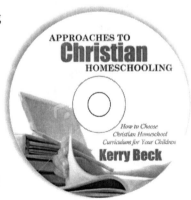

http://HowToHomeschoolMyChild.com/ approaches-resources

RANGER PRESS RESOURCES

HowToHomeschoolMyChild.com/ranger-press

Everything You Want to Know About Homeschooling
{FREE for you} HowToHomeschoolMyChild.com

Raising Leaders, Not Followers (Christian Leadership Series #1)
Most homeschoolers continue to offer their children the same type of education they received; they just do it at home. Parents prepare their children in a public school-grade level fashion for a future job, teaching them only "what to think". Our founding fathers received something different – a leadership education through mentoring. Leadership education trains our children "how to think" in a variety of situations.

Kerry Beck discuss three types of educational models, how to move from "what to think" to "how to think" in your homeschool and practical ways to implement a Biblical Leadership Education from young kids to young adults.

Teach Your Children "How to Think" with Mentoring
(Christian Leadership Series #2)
Go beyond the early years of training leaders and learn how to provide self-directed study for your own children. Mentoring has been the successful model to train statesmen, entrepreneurs and community leaders.

Discover clues to becoming a successful mentor to your children and to offer your children opportunities to study their own interests.

Don't be fooled by the conveyor-belt model! We all learn more when we are self-motivated to study. Use mentoring this coming year to encourage your own children to be self-motivated in their studies.

Hop Off the Conveyor Belt: Tips & Stories (Christian Leadership Series #3)

Real-life stories compiled from homeschool moms – tips, tricks & real-life stories of what worked and what didn't.

Star of Bethlehem Family Study Guide

The Study is Called Star of Bethlehem Bible Study Ebook. Not only is there a fresh focus on God's AWESOME communication with us throughout time, but you will learn more astronomy than YEARS of study in a text! Kerry takes you deeply into the Word of God to dig out what God has to say about stars, astronomy, astrology, and neatest of all, how God used STARS to tell about His plan for salvation through Jesus Christ!

Skies of the Cross Family Study Guide

Many wonders occurred the day Jesus died. Spend time as a family discovering when, what & how all the wonders. Besides Easter Bible verses, what will you discover in our guide? Clues about Christ's Crucifixion, Prophecies Fulfilled at the Cross, Timing of the Day of the Cross, Blood Moons Today, Solar & Lunar Eclipses, How God Uses the Skies as a Sign

Christmas Celebrations: Advent, Christmas & Epiphany

Keep Christ the center of your holiday celebrations as you learn Biblical ways to celebrate 3 special times of year.

Christmas Around the World

Discover how other countries celebrate Christmas with hands-on activities and lesson plans already created for you.

ABOUT THE AUTHOR

After 10 years of homeschooling (her kids have graduated), she enjoys meeting with moms to encourage them in raising, educating and encouraging their own kids. She also has a strong desire to show families how to give their children a love of learning. Kerry loves being a mom and loves homeschooling. Sit back and let her help YOU . . . as you give your kids the best education, a superb, Christian education, where they will love learning, as well as be able to think critically & Biblically.

Kerry has been married to Stephen for 31 years. Together they raised three kids. Ashley is married to Jesse and stays at home with their children. Gentry is married to Andrew and works in event planning. Hunter graduated from Texas A&M and works for a management consulting firm.

Kerry shares fun activities to use in your homeschooling and would love to connect with you online:

Blog: http://HowToHomeschoolMyChild.com/blog
Facebook: http://facebook.com/HowToHomeschoolMyChild
Twitter: http://twitter.com/kerrybeck
Pinterest: http://pinterest.com/HowToHomeschool
email: Kerry@HowToHomeschoolMyChild.com

SPEAKING

If you are looking for a speaker about homeschooling, please contact Kerry at Kerry@HowToHomeschoolMyChild.com or call (979)703-5724. You can read more about her speaking topics here:

http://HowToHomeschoolMyChild.com/resources/speaking

CPSIA information can be obtained
at www.ICGtesting.com
Printed in the USA
FFOW02n0308290817
39328FF